HOW TO DO
A SCIENCE
FAIR PROJECT

HOW TO DO A SCIENCE FAIR PROJECT

SALVATORE TOCCI

AN EXPERIMENTAL
SCIENCE SERIES BOOK

A GROLIER COMPANY

FRANKLIN WATTS
NEW YORK / LONDON
TORONTO / SYDNEY / 1986

Diagrams by Vantage Art

Photographs courtesy of the author: pp. 16, 17, 21, 26, 30, 36, 42, 48, 53, 55, 56, 62, 65, 102, 103, 108, 115; UPI/Bettmann Newsphotos: pp. 31, 35; Argonne National Laboratory: p. 32; Photo-Researchers: p. 33; AP/Wide World: p. 34.

Library of Congress Cataloging-in-Publication Data

Tocci, Salvatore.
How to do a science fair project.

(An Experimental science series book)
Bibliography: p.
Includes index.
Summary: A step-by-step guide for creating a variety of projects suitable for entry in a science fair with suggestions for choosing a subject, performing the experiment, and polishing the presentation.
1. Science—Experiments—Juvenile literature. 2. Science—Exhibitions—Juvenile literature. [1. Science—Experiments. 2. Science—Exhibitions. 3. Experiments] I. Title. II. Series.
Q164.T68 1986   507'.2   86-9239
ISBN 0-531-15123-9 (paper ed.) — ISBN 0-531-10245-9 (lib. bdg.)

CONTENTS

For Mary Jo

INTRODUCTION
WHAT IS A SCIENCE
FAIR PROJECT?

Doing a science fair project is a good way to learn about science and how scientists think and work. You may think that science consists mainly of factual information contained in some book and that scientists always make their discoveries by following a set routine. You may even believe that science is primarily limited to schools, libraries, and research laboratories. But science is more than a subject taught in school, the topic of books in libraries, or a procedure followed in a laboratory. Science is a search for answers.

One of the best ways for you to become involved in such a search is to conduct a science fair project. This book will show you how to carry out a project and explain how scientists approach problems in searching for some answer or discovery. All you need to get started is a good idea and some curiosity. The only limits on what you can accomplish might be those of your imagination.

This book will discuss each step you will follow, from selecting a topic to presenting your project at a science fair. Although this book covers the kinds of projects usually done for a science fair, the emphasis is on projects dealing with original investigations in which you must conduct experiments to answer a question. Chapters 4 and 5 contain information and suggestions only for projects involving original investigations. These projects require more thought and effort than those limited to collecting information from encyclopedias or building a model from a store-bought kit.

No matter what kind of project you choose, what you learn will make you more knowledgeable about the world and how it works. Your project may even win an award. But beware—although you may heed all the advice and suggestions offered in this book, you may still face disappointments, get trapped in blind alleys, or follow misleading clues. Yet that's what a science fair project is all about—the real world.

Unfortunately, some science fair projects look like class assignments rather than the tangible output of a fertile imagination and a serious investigation into the real world. You may be planning to do a project since it is a required part of your science course. A certain percentage of your grade may even depend on your project. With little time and practically no preparation, you might resort to constructing a poster display of pictures cut from magazines, writing a report from an encyclopedia, or performing a lab exercise obtained from a textbook. Such projects are not real science but only "cookbook" chemistry—just follow the recipe, and the result is guaranteed.

Even if your science fair project is a required assignment, try to approach it with enthusiasm and a desire to discover something about the world. Follow the suggestions in this book to make the assignment a learning experience. Since science involves challenges to be faced and solutions to be discovered, a science fair project should reflect a sense of excitement, as well as creativity, curiosity, and achievement.

If you think about these qualities, you'll see why a scientist can be considered a detective. Both are looking for an answer, with only a few ideas or clues leading the way to the final solution. By conducting a science project that seeks to answer a question raised by curiosity, you'll be carrying out the same mental processes used in detective work.

To see the connection between conducting a science fair project and a criminal investigation, you may want to read one of the books listed in the bibliography, that shows how scientists have used detective work in solving some baffling problems. But to appreciate the full extent to which detective work can be applied to your project, you should read about one of the world's greatest detectives, Sherlock Holmes. Holmes's investigations were always challenges in which the solutions were found by using a logical, scientific process, much like the one needed to carry out a science fair project. Before undertaking your project, you might find it worthwhile to read about some of Holmes's cases in *The Complete Sherlock Holmes.*

1

SELECTING

A TOPIC

Once you've decided to do a science fair project, you need to select a topic. If you look no further than your science textbook for ideas, choosing a topic can be difficult. In fact, selecting a topic can be the most challenging part of your project. The challenge may seem difficult, especially if you don't know where to begin.

Start by imitating Holmes—depend upon your ability to observe. When Holmes meets Dr. Watson for the first time, he tells him, "Observation with me is second nature." Holmes proves his point by telling Watson what he knows about him simply by observing his physical appearance: Watson is a doctor who has undergone recent hardship and sickness while serving with the British army in Afghanistan. If Holmes can make so much from a quick observation, think what you can learn from a more thorough one.

WHERE TO OBSERVE

Start by observing the world around you, and you'll find all sorts of interesting phenomena that can provide ideas for a project. This might involve visiting a museum, looking under the kitchen sink, walking through the forest, watching a movie, or going to the zoo. Look closely and be alert for the unexpected. Ideas for a project can arise without warning. Many important discoveries have been made because scientists have taken notice of something totally unexpected. Perhaps the best-known unexpected finding in the history of science was the discovery of penicillin.

In 1928, Alexander Fleming was working with bacterial cultures. Absorbed in his project, Fleming didn't bother to clean the culture dishes after he had finished with them but instead allowed them to collect. Mold soon started to form in these dishes. Even though his attention was focused on his work, Fleming observed that the areas surrounding the mold in these dishes were free of bacterial growth.

Fleming reasoned the mold contained a chemical substance that inhibited the growth and reproduction of bacteria. He abandoned his original project to investigate his new idea. Fleming confirmed his suspicion when he placed samples of the mold in different media and found no bacterial growth. Fleming's keen observation and interest in pursuing an unexpected finding led to the discovery of an antibiotic that was to save thousands of lives during World War II and millions thereafter.

OBSERVE CLOSELY
AND CAREFULLY

Don't underestimate the importance of making observations. Observation plays a fundamental role in science, as well as in detective work. Many young scientists, however, fail to recognize that observation can be an extremely complex activity capable of revealing much information. If you want to test your powers of observation, perform a simple experiment that requires only a candle, match, and ruler. Describe the candle as completely as possible; then light it and make additional observations.

Do not confuse observations with interpretations. You are making an observation if you say that a colorless liquid collects near the wick. But if you say this liquid is melted wax, you are making an interpretation. See how many *observations* you can make. Observe closely, since you may overlook something if you don't pay close attention.

PURSUE YOUR INTERESTS

Focus your observations on something that genuinely interests you. Holmes once answered Dr. Watson's question regarding whether any cases were open for investigation by saying, "Some ten or twelve, but none which present any feature of interest. They are important, you understand, without being interesting." Do not select a topic on the basis of its importance to others but rather on its interest and appeal to *you*. After all, you will be spending considerable time on the project, so you might as well enjoy what you are doing.

Look at your favorite hobby for a science project idea. A model-railroad buff could design and assemble a better transformer. Perhaps your pet or some sport might inspire you. A tropical fish enthusiast could develop a more efficient filtering system, or study fish behavior under different lighting conditions. A tennis player might want to design a stronger racket. In any case, consider your personal interests.

OTHER SOURCES OF IDEAS

If your hobbies fail to provide any ideas for a project, don't give up—there are many other places to search.

A hobby such as model railroading might provide an idea for your project.

Other sources for ideas are books, magazines, encyclopedias, special publications, television shows, and people.

Glance through your science textbook to review the topics you covered in class. Did you find a particular chapter interesting, or did you do exceptionally well in one area of the course? Reread those sections in the book to refresh your memory and perhaps provide the spark for a creative idea. While reading the chapter, remember you are looking for ideas. Pay particular attention to topics in which research is currently being conducted or where problems remain to be solved. Refer to the end of the chapter for any ideas for independent investigations or suggestions for further readings.

Another source for ideas is a library. Check the card catalog for titles of science books. Don't be limited to titles that sound like textbooks; check out those with provocative titles like *Psychic Phenomena* or *Creatures beneath the Seas*. These books may deal more with fancy than fact, but they may inspire you. For example, many scientists are trying to establish the scientific basis for extrasensory perception (ESP). Others are looking for deep-sea organisms that may be the ancestors of modern fish. If you head in this direction, make sure your idea for a project is scientifically sound and does not fall into the area of pseudoscience.

If you have no success with books, ask your librarian for assistance in locating magazines that can pro-

Books, magazines, and encyclopedias in your school library can help you get ideas for a project.

vide ideas. Possibilities include *Scientific American,* *Science News, Discover, Science World, Omni,* and *Popular Science.* Numerous scientific journals and publications are available that provide current information on a wide variety of topics.

Also check the *Reader's Guide to Periodical Literature,* an index containing lists of articles published in many magazines. Listing the author's last name, title of the article, and a short synopsis, this guide will direct you to the specific volume and pages of the magazine where the article appeared. In some cases, your school library may not have the magazine on file; a trip to a college library may be necessary.

Some of the professional scientific journals may be too advanced for you to understand the material. On the other hand, you may find some publications too "sensational." In either case, try to scan these magazines to see if you can pick up some project ideas without worrying about all the details or being distracted by the sensationalism.

For example, a recent magazine story reported on new and rather unusual methods for making a visit to the dentist less painful. These methods included applying mild electric currents to the ears and hands of the patient and providing video games and comedy films in the waiting room. But many dentists question the effectiveness of these methods and claim they do nothing to help their patients. What do you think? Perhaps you could contact your dentist to discuss these approaches and explore ideas for a project.

ADDITIONAL LIBRARY SOURCES

Encyclopedias provide general information about many topics. Articles in *The Encyclopaedia Britannica* are detailed and written by specialists in their fields. The *Encyclopaedia Americana* is a good source of various aspects of technology. *Collier's Encyclopedia* is probably the most up-to-date encyclopedia, containing the latest information on scientific advances. *The World Book Encyclopedia* actually lists project ideas with some of the science articles. *McGraw-Hill Encyclopedia of Science & Technology* specializes in science, mathematics, and engineering and is the most technical of these books.

If these encyclopedias do not inspire you, ask your librarian for help in tracking down other sources for project ideas. Your librarian can assist you with checking indexes, microfilms, and microfiches. These last two sources contain photographic records of many publications and require a special viewer because of the small size of the print.

CHECK PAST SCIENCE FAIR PROJECTS

Check publications and pamphlets describing past science fair projects for project ideas. Each year Science Service (1719 N Street, N.W., Washington, DC 20036) publishes the abstracts from the International Science and Engineering Fair (ISEF). The abstracts are short descriptions of the projects entered in the ISEF. Science Service also has information on the Science Talent Search for Westinghouse Science Scholarships and Awards. A winning project in this competition can lead to a scholarship that will cover four years of college expenses! Abstracts of past projects may also be available from local, regional, and state science fairs.

Although reading about past projects may sound boring, it is just the opposite. *Science Service Abstracts* in particular is a gold mine. If this publication doesn't lead you to several ideas, it will at least show you how ingenious other students have been. This is bound to propel you to new and greater heights!

Don't hesitate to build upon the work of others. Many scientific achievements have their roots in the past. For example, vaccination against diseases such as measles and polio was not possible until a method was developed for growing viruses in glass flasks where they could be studied. Once this technique was perfected, scientists could explore the development of vaccines against viral diseases.

Another scientific discovery with its roots in the past was the process by which sperm and egg cells are produced. Once scientists understood how nonsex cells divided, they predicted the process by which sperm and egg cells were formed even before they actually observed it! Obviously, previous scientific investigations had laid the foundation for new discoveries.

EDUCATIONAL TELEVISION SHOWS

How many times have your parents told you to turn off the television and do your homework? Here's your chance to do your homework by watching television! There are several shows that might provide you with an idea for a project. Check a newspaper or guide for a listing of upcoming telecasts. Pay particular attention to shows like NOVA, National Geographic, Wild Kingdom, COSMOS, Nature, and to any scientific special produced for the Public Broadcasting System.

Many of these shows feature recent advances in scientific knowledge. They often interview scientists who are carrying out projects in medicine, engineering, space exploration, animal behavior, oceanography, computer technology, and genetics. The producers of the show will sometimes supply a script and additional resource materials, including background information and questions needing further study.

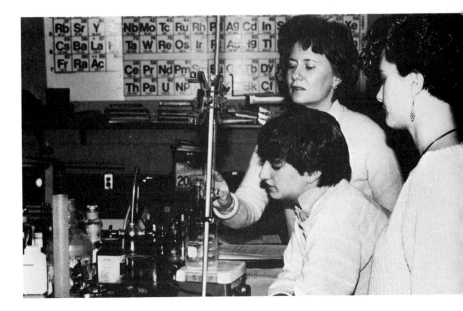

Don't forget to talk to science teachers in
your school for help in finding a topic.

TALK WITH SOMEONE

If you still aren't sure what you want to do for a project, you may want to talk with professionals such as scientists, doctors, veterinarians, nurses, engineers, or teachers. They can be found at hospitals, universities, government agencies, environmental organizations, zoos, museums, industries, computer centers, pharmaceutical companies, greenhouses, observatories, botanical gardens, pharmacies, and water treatment plants, all listed in your telephone directory.

These professionals are usually eager to help young scientists and may give special assistance if your project is in their area of expertise. But their time may be limited, so call or write a few weeks in advance to ask for an appointment. State what information you want to obtain and request copies of any written materials available on the topic. Before the interview, prepare your questions; during the interview, take notes or tape-record the conversation. Obtain permission before taping the interview. Follow up the interview with a letter, thanking the person for their time and assistance.

If you cannot meet with a professional, perhaps a teacher can arrange for a brainstorming session between you and other interested students to explore ideas and suggestions for projects. The group may find it helpful to begin by talking about mutual interests, possibly starting with courses you enjoyed or field trips you found interesting.

FEATURES OF A GOOD TOPIC

Make sure your project idea is realistic and can be accomplished with available resources. You may be interested in atomic structure (a topic on which many books have been written), but you will not be able to probe certain mysteries of the atom without a particle accelerator, found in only several laboratories in the world.

Your selection of a topic will be limited by your access to the equipment and materials required to conduct your project. In addition, you may require live specimens, chemicals, measuring devices, and special lab apparatus. Check your school science laboratory to see what equipment and supplies are available. A nearby research facility or industry may have specialized equipment not found in schools. For example, you may be able to get access to an X-ray machine to irradiate specimens, a high-speed centrifuge to create ultragravitational forces, or a powerful telescope to observe the stars.

If the project can be accomplished with available resources, remember that *you* will have to do it! You may occasionally require advice and suggestions from a teacher or professional scientist, but the project must reflect your ideas and efforts. Be sure you can wrestle with the topic by yourself, with only periodic support from others. If you plan to submit your project for evaluation in a science fair competition, you will be judged on *your* knowledge and input into the investigation. Little credit for initiative and creativity can be given to someone whose project reflects the work and ideas of others.

Finally, be sure that you will have enough time to complete the project. Don't select a topic that is too broad or generalized. Not only will you have difficulty in planning the project, but you will also lack the time to arrive at any conclusions or results.

After choosing your topic, narrow it down to a specific question or problem that can be solved within a reasonable time. Too often students end up with poor project results because they failed to focus on a specific question or problem when choosing a topic.

CAN YOU IDENTIFY A GOOD TOPIC WHEN YOU SEE ONE?

You might find it helpful to examine the following list to determine which ones would make a suitable science fair project. Why are some of these suggested topics not appropriate for a project? Can you suggest improvements or changes that would make these titles more likely to lead to a successful science fair project?

Is There Life on Mars?
Working with Plants
Effects of Radiation on the Growth of Geraniums

The World of Insects
Regeneration of Limbs in Salamanders
Determination of the Radii of Subatomic Particles
Measuring the Efficiency of Solar Collectors
Courtship Behaviors of African Wildlife
Methods of Web Construction in House Spiders
A Seashell Collection from Three
 Caribbean Islands
Principles of Aerodynamics
A Method to Increase the Fruit Yield
 of Banana Trees
Recombinant DNA Technology
Estimating Chemical Bond Angles from Nuclear
 Magnetic Resonance
Which Antacid Is Best?
The Effects of Acid Rain
Eye Pigmentation and Mating Behavior
 of Fruit Flies

Some titles are too vague: "Working with Plants," "The World of Insects," "Principles of Aerodynamics," "Recombinant DNA Technology," and "The Effects of Acid Rain." Left as they are, these titles do not provide a good idea of where to begin. For example, you would have a better idea of where to start if you changed "Working with Plants" to "How the Moisture Content of Soil Affects the Growth of Tomatoes." The latter is far more specific.

Other titles are beyond the capability of being accomplished with available resources: "Is There Life on Mars?" and "Courtship Behaviors of African Wildlife." You could not undertake these projects unless you had unlimited funds, access to highly sophisticated equipment, or months of free time.

Two of these titles might be beyond the capabilities of a young scientist: "Determining the Radii of

Subatomic Particles" and "Estimating Chemical Bond Angles from Nuclear Magnetic Resonance." These projects require highly sophisticated equipment and technical knowledge. In the end, such projects may not reflect *your* thinking and effort but rather those of a professional scientist.

The remaining titles represent better ideas since they are more specific, realistic, and capable of being accomplished within a reasonable time. If you picked the last title, you made a good choice—this is the title of an award-winning project. A brief look at this project might help you see what steps to follow in selecting a good topic.

AN AWARD-WINNING IDEA

As a high school freshman, Kaushik Bhaumik developed a keen interest in biology. In his sophomore year, he wanted to do a science fair project. He talked to a friend who was investigating the chemistry of eye pigmentation in a fruit fly with the scientific name *Drosophila melanogaster*. Noticing Kaushik's interest, his friend gave him an article on eye pigmentation in fruit flies. Kaushik began to get an idea for his project.

Fascinated by the wide variety of interesting eye colors, Kaushik sought additional information on what was known about eye pigmentation in *Drosophila*. After he did some reading at a local college library and talked with a teacher in his school, Kaushik began to question whether any connection existed between eye pigmentation and some aspect of the fly's behavior.

Notice the steps Kaushik took to get a topic for his project: talking to a friend, reading library materials, and checking with a teacher. Only then could he choose a topic: does any pattern exist between eye pigmentation and mating behavior in the fruit fly?

Kaushik Bhaumik talked to a friend, read some magazine articles, and checked with his science teacher before selecting his topic.

From his readings of the scientific literature, Kaushik discovered some evidence suggesting such a relationship. Once he was assured that he could obtain the necessary specimens, equipment, and materials, he began his project.

By the way, if you think you might do another project at some future time, choose a topic that can produce several ideas to explore. For example, Kaushik began with a project examining the relationship between eye pigmentation and mating behavior. He concluded from his results that as eye pigmentation increased from no pigment (white eyes) to full pigmentation (red eyes), the success of matings also increased.

Once he established this relationship, Kaushik next questioned if a connection also existed between mating behavior and wing patterns. In his second project, he discovered a relationship between mating behavior and the sound frequencies produced by different wing patterns. His third project is to attempt to control mating behavior by producing particular sound waves. This technique might help farmers control fruit fly infestations without the use of pesticides.

WARNING—SOME TOPICS REQUIRE SPECIAL CONSIDERATIONS

Most science fairs have rules and regulations concerning certain projects. In some cases, you may have to modify or change your topic because of these rules. To save yourself a lot of unnecessary work, find out the rules even before you start looking for ideas. The following three rules are part of most science fair regulations:

First, any *vertebrates* (animals with backbones, such as fish, frogs, birds, and mammals) used in a project must be given every humane consideration for their comfort and treatment. Whenever possible, use plants, single-celled organisms, or *invertebrates* (animals without backbones, such as worms, insects, crabs, and jellyfish). In fact, invertebrates make excellent test subjects. However, if your project requires the use of vertebrates, you must have adequate knowledge about their behavior, characteristics, needs, and handling.

Proof of qualified adult supervision, from a teacher or research scientist, may be required by some science fair competitions before accepting a project involving vertebrates. Any project involving inhumane treatment cannot be included in a science fair.

Such projects raise moral and ethical questions. You must also follow recommended methods for sacrificing animals if this is required to conduct your project. Contact Science Service for additional information on projects involving vertebrates.

Second, check with Science Service if your project will involve human subjects. Some science fairs prohibit the use of human subjects. Again, supervision by a qualified person is required if such a project is done. These guidelines also apply even if you plan to be the subject of your own project.

Third, a project involving genetic engineering must be carried out within well-defined guidelines. Genetic engineering is a recent scientific breakthrough in which the genes, composed of a chemical substance called DNA, can be altered or rearranged. If your project involves genetic engineering, only research normally conducted in a microbiological laboratory without the use of special containment facilities is permitted. The supervision of a qualified scientist is also required. Write the National Institute of Health (9000 Rockville, Bethesda, Maryland 20892) for information on experiments involving genetic engineering.

As Holmes tells Dr. Watson, "You did not know where to look, and so you missed all that was important." You now should know where to look for ideas and recognize some important factors to consider when selecting a topic.

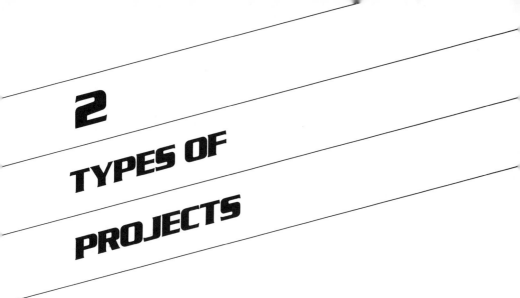

2
TYPES OF PROJECTS

Once you have selected a topic, your next step is to examine the various ways you can conduct your project. The type of project you decide to undertake will affect how you should proceed with your work. Nearly all science fair projects fall into one of five categories: assembling a model, constructing a display, carrying out a survey, repeating someone else's work, or undertaking an original investigation.

MODELS

Models are the format of choice for many elementary and junior high school students. With easy-to-use materials such as wood, metal, and cardboard, you can construct a model easily and quickly. Examples include a model of the solar system, the human eye, a frog's internal organs, and a volcano.

Such models may be detailed and colorful, but building them rarely draws upon your thinking, reasoning, or creative skills. In fact, models based on textbook drawings or built from kits are not allowed in some science fairs held for junior high and high school students. These models are excluded since they do not reflect any originality or an attempt to explore a project the way a scientist would.

For such science fairs, an acceptable model must include some original thinking, be a creative solution to an old problem, or constitute a more efficient system. Adding flashing lights or colorful labels reflects little originality. Thousands of projects have featured models of volcanoes complete with "fire" and flowing "lava." Year after year, such models fail to impress the judges at science fair competitions. If you want to construct a model, try to build one that displays creativity or has a practical application.

Show your creativity if you build a model. Here a garbage can is used as part of a solar energy project.

Two graduate students test their model of a solar-powered airship built from plastic sheeting, weather balloons, wood, wire, and string.

For example, a model of the human eye constructed from a textbook illustration lacks any original input. However, a working model of a device that translates electrical impulses into Braille characters might have applications for blind people. A model of a jet aircraft is uninspiring, but a model of a plane that is aerodynamically more efficient and uses less fuel than a conventional jet might be interesting to flight engineers. A model of a robot is simple to construct by following the assembly instructions. Yet, a model of a robot controlled by a microcomputer and using a program you wrote might be an award-winning project.

A scale model of the first nuclear reactor

ROLE OF MODELS IN SCIENCE

Models have played a major role in some important scientific discoveries. Scientists have used pieces of wood, plastic, and metal to construct models of atoms, chemical compounds, and cellular structures. Today many scientists are using computers to create models, not only of the submicroscopic world but also of the cosmos.

In building models, scientists rely upon information gathered from various sources. For example, they can test their ideas to check out data obtained from lab investigations. In some cases, these models were so successful that the scientists received a Nobel Prize, the highest level of recognition in their field.

Perhaps the best-known example in which a model played a critical role was the discovery of the structure of the chemical compound known as DNA. Based on previous experiments, scientists knew that DNA was responsible for hereditary characteristics such as the color of your eyes or the curliness of your hair. Although they had identified all the components in DNA, scientists did not know how all these pieces were arranged. Three scientists, James Watson, Francis Crick, and Maurice Wilkins, attacked this problem by building models. They finally succeeded in building a model that correctly showed the arrangement of all the pieces. In 1962, they received a Nobel Prize for their work.

James Watson (left) and Francis Crick won a Nobel Prize for their discovery, with Maurice Wilkins, of the structure of the DNA molecule, a model of which is shown here.

Buckminster Fuller, inventor of the geodesic dome, shown with a model of his "Tensegrity" sphere. Fuller claimed this design could be used for a giant sphere so light and strong it could support a floating space station a mile (about 1.5 kilometers) in diameter.

Models can also be a creative outlet for your imagination. Consider the work of the famous engineer and architect Buckminster Fuller. In the 1920s, Fuller began using special metals known as alloys to build unconventional structures. He experimented with various models before constructing his first geodesic dome, a structure consisting of triangular parts made of lightweight metal. Fuller designed more than 2000 geodesic domes, found today in more than thirty countries.

Engineers are constantly building models to test for more efficient designs of cars, planes, and other machines. They often use computers to build such models. If you are interested in doing a project on computer modeling, check what computers are available in your school. You should also learn how to use graphic tablets and drawing pads. These devices will make it much easier to produce drawings on the computer screen.

High school senior Ocie Beacham displays a model of a jet plane he designed. The material is cardboard.

*Graphics tablets and drawing pads will make
your job easier if you want to produce drawings
on a computer screen. Programs are available
to "dump" these drawings on a printer.*

DISPLAYS

Another type of project is a display that mixes specimens, photographs, drawings, and written reports in
some combination. A display can be attractive and
contain a good deal of scientific information.

Suppose you decide to conduct a project tracing
the history of flight. Pictures of the first flight by the
Wright brothers, photographs of different jet aircraft,
and written information on the space shuttle can be
arranged into an attractive display. The visual and
written information displayed in your project could
provide an impressive summary of the history of avi-
ation.

A display can also reflect a hobby or some leisure time activity. For example, an interesting arrangement of rocks, butterflies, or leaves would make an attractive display.

By now, however, you should realize that a display, like model building, can be quite elaborate but very unoriginal. Whether the display represents a hobby or a collection gathered on field trips, adding some scientific information about the items would be valuable.

Perhaps you can show some originality by trying to discover several interesting scientific facts about your collection. Rather than showing all your butterflies, try selecting any that have striking resemblances. Even though two butterflies have been placed in separate categories of classification, they may be similar in coloration, wing structure, or body shape. Your project can explore the scientific reason why these specimens were placed in separate classification groups. Perhaps you can extend your project into an investigation of living butterflies, both in nature and under controlled laboratory conditions. You may arrive at some interesting observations that can then become part of your project.

As opposed to displaying all the leaves collected from trees in your backyard or neighborhood, a project using leaves exposed to different environmental conditions would be more interesting. Check with environmental groups to determine if any threat to your local community exists, such as acid rain, industrial air pollution, or chemical waste disposal. These problems are quite serious in some areas of the country; a scientific examination of the local foliage may reveal some hidden impact on your community. In any case, a project involving a scientific look into the materials on display would be more impressive than simply mounting and identifying the specimens.

SURVEYS

Newspapers, magazines, television stations, and manufacturers often conduct polls to determine people's opinions on various topics, shows, or products. On the basis of contacting from several hundred to no more than a few thousand people, a candidate is considered unbeatable, a television show is canceled, or a new soft drink is introduced to the consumer market. Obviously, surveys can have a tremendous impact on society.

Surveys can also be the basis for your science fair project. You can survey almost anything, from the types of bacteria growing in your school to the kinds of dogs living in your town. Naturally, the larger in scope the survey, the more thorough you must be in your planning. Be sure the size and composition of the population surveyed are adequate. You can make valid conclusions from relatively small sample sizes only if the individuals being surveyed are a representative cross-section of the population. If only a few individuals are surveyed, any conclusion you reach regarding the total population might not be valid. Just think if you asked your friends what sports they liked or songs they enjoyed. Your friends' responses may be to your liking but may not represent common opinion.

A survey may lead to other scientific processes that can become part of your project. Before drawing any conclusions from your survey, you may need to use mathematics to analyze your results. If you do, learn some *statistics*, a branch of mathematics that deals with the collection, analysis, and interpretation of a large amount of data. Check the section "Analyzing Your Results" in Chapter 7 for a brief discussion of a few statistical procedures. You can also talk to your math teacher to learn which procedures might be useful in analyzing the results of your survey.

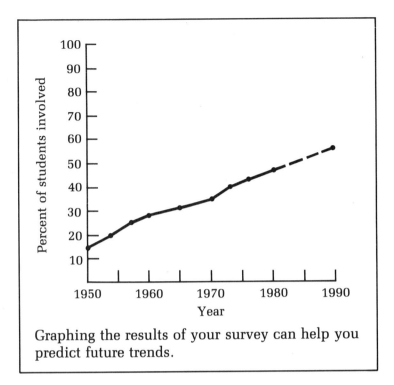

Graphing the results of your survey can help you predict future trends.

Graphs, data tables, and written reports can also be part of your survey. The results of your survey, if conducted over a period of time, may even enable you to make a scientific prediction about future trends. Predictions concerning human behavior are commonly made and can yield interesting results. You may want to survey the patterns of eating behavior among students in different grade levels in your school. Do types of food, number of meals and snacks eaten, preferences for fast foods, and diet regimens vary among different ages or genders? If you survey patterns of eating behavior, can you make any prediction as to what fast food will be the most popular next year?

[39]

In addition to eating, many other behavior patterns are constantly changing among students. Working with a teacher, you could develop a questionnaire that explores patterns of social behavior in your school. Do students in your school enjoy the same sports, gather at a particular place to socialize, watch certain television shows, or have similar hobbies? Remember that many science fairs have regulations regarding the use of human subjects in projects, so be sure to check these rules.

REPEATS FROM THE PAST

Some projects repeat a classic experiment or demonstration found in a textbook, lab manual, or book such as *Classic Papers in Genetics, Great Scientific Experiments: Twenty Experiments That Changed Our View of the World, Great Scientists Speak Again,* or *Experiments in Chemistry.* See the bibliography for the names of the authors and publishers of these books.

As with models and displays, such a project may involve little or no creativity. Try to add something original, perhaps demonstrating some practical application. Take the classic experiment performed by the chemist Jacques Charles in 1787. He found that all gases expand by the same fraction of their original volume when they are heated over the same temperature range. If you check a chemistry textbook, you'll discover that you could repeat his experiment with a piece of glass tubing and a drop of mercury. But to be more creative (and avoid working with mercury, which is toxic), demonstrate the application of Charles' law to hot-air balloons. Can you design a balloon that operates more efficiently when the heated air expands according to Charles' law?

Perhaps you can approach a classic experiment from a different angle. Review the work of Gregor

Mendel. His experiments with pea plants in the 1860s were the first carefully planned investigations in genetics. All you need to repeat his experiments are pea plants, a place to grow them, and lots of time. Mendel took years to perform his genetic studies. He analyzed seven hereditary characteristics in pea plants, but you can save time by doing just one. But you can save even more time by writing a computer program that summarizes all his work.

By the way, notice how simple equipment and a few materials (glass tube, drop of mercury, and pea plants) were used to make major scientific discoveries. Perhaps your project may require less than you think.

ORIGINAL INVESTIGATIONS

Conducting a classic experiment might pave the way for the final type of project: an original investigation. If you repeat Mendel's work with garden peas, you may become so intrigued by heredity that you'll decide to do a project in genetics on a plant species about which little is known. Similarly, Charles's work can be the basis for a space shuttle project: How does the absence of gravity affect the behavior of gases when they are heated?

Be aware that an original investigation is often the most difficult to plan and conduct. An investigative project usually requires more library research, critical thinking, and laboratory work than the other types of projects. If you are interested only in perfecting your skills in model building or assembling a display, then a project from one of the first four categories would be appropriate.

However, if your ambition is to understand how scientists often approach problems, then you should do an original investigation. In this case, you will have

A project involving an original investigation requires careful preparation before you begin your laboratory work.

to think of an original idea, perform experiments, collect information, and arrive at a conclusion. Since this type of project requires more work, you should not find it surprising that most entries at science fairs fall within the first four categories.

SOME OTHER REASONS FOR DOING A NONINVESTIGATIVE PROJECT

Consider some valid reasons why one of the first four categories may be more suited to your needs before tackling an investigative project. If you are planning to enter your first science fair, a display or model may be a better way to become acquainted with the steps necessary to complete a project. Constructing a model can be a learning experience and a way of "getting your feet wet" in all aspects of a science project. Also, if your background in science is not especially strong or extensive, you may be more comfortable with a project involving a survey or display rather than an original investigation.

A noninvestigative project can also create an awareness and appreciation for science, revealing its nature as fully as an investigative project. You can appreciate the importance of a noninvestigative project by examining the work of Charles Darwin, especially his studies done on the Galapagos Islands.

"Evolution" might very well be the first word that comes into your mind when you think of Darwin. His theory of natural selection is one of the major unifying themes in biology, applying to all types of organisms. Yet Darwin also explored heredity, the growth of plants, the formation of atolls, and many other scientific pursuits. But many of Darwin's important discoveries and valuable contributions did not come from experiments, but rather from his ability to observe nature and ask questions.

Darwin spent five years as a naturalist aboard a ship, traveling around the world. His curiosity led him to explore the mysteries hidden from the casual observer or the uninterested spectator. He collected large numbers of specimens, from barnacles to birds, and then proceeded to describe them in detail, marveling at their great diversity. Darwin's curiosity led him to develop an interest in science that grew in both scope and depth. Much of his work did not depend upon original investigations, yet all scientists recognize the value of his studies.

Like Darwin, you may want to explore the world around you. Construct a model of the moon, demonstrate how tides form, or collect and classify organisms that live in your local pond. These projects do not involve the experimental procedures usually followed in an investigative project. They will, however, require you to observe, explore, question, and describe just as Darwin did. This type of project might even lead you to ask some question that can be answered only with an original investigation.

PROJECT CATEGORIES

Examine the following titles to get an idea of the wide range of possibilities for projects. Included are ideas for models, displays, surveys, and both repetitive and original investigations. These titles are from projects submitted at a recent ISEF, the largest science fair in terms of states and countries represented. The ISEF includes projects in behavioral and social sciences, computer science, engineering, earth and space sciences, mathematics, medicine and health, and zoology.

Moods and Music
Optical Illusions: Do You See What I See?
Morality in Children
Chemistry and the Personal Computer:
    Does the Computer Enhance Learning?
A Smart Pill in Our Future?
Artificial Embryo
Computers and Society
Teaching Sign Language with a Computer
Motion of the Ocean
Can an Apple Computer Recognize Speech?
Magical Numbers and Series
Soap-Film Math
Physics of Twisting and Somersaulting
What Is the Best Load for a 7mm
    Magnum Rifle?
The Real Reason Airplanes Fly
Extending the Life of Ordinary Light Bulbs
Artificial Intelligence: Logic of the Mind

ANOTHER LIST

If you decide to do an original investigation, there are numerous areas you can explore. Examine the following list for ideas. You can change any title to match your interests.

Three-Year Study: Effect of Color on Mice
Effects of Stress on Alcohol Consumption
    in Mice
Effects of Colors and Word Ordering on Memory
Biochemical Changes in Seeds after Germination
Optimizing Hydrogen Photoproduced by
    Marine Algae
Meat Tenderizers: Study of Enzyme Activity
Comparison of Sugar Content in Soft Drinks
Comparative Study of the Fertilizer of Some
    Marine Algae
Factors Affecting the Growth of Geranium Cells
Effects of Microwaves on Seed Germination
Using Electricity to Control the Direction of
    Root Growth
STOP! You May Be Using the Wrong Detergent!
Comparative Studies of the Deterioration of
    Vitamin C in Various Samples
Design, Construction, and Efficiency Analysis of
    a Solar Pond
Effects of Outboard Motor Exhaust on Selected
    Marine Organisms
Five-Year Acid Rain Analysis through Various
    Studies
Can Dandelions Be Used to Measure
    Lead Pollution in Soil?
Effects of Thirst Quenchers and Exercise on
    Blood Pressure
Vitamin D and Its Effects on Rats
Effect of Bee Toxin on Rheumatoid Arthritis

How Antiseptics Affect Bacteria
Salad Bowl Microorganisms
Sage: A Natural Preservative
Food Preferences of Wild Birds
Effects of Magnetism on the Regeneration
    of Planaria
How Alcohol Affects Chicken Embryos
Pollution: Effects of Copper on Oysters
Effects of Ultrasound on Growth and
    Development
Tumor Inhibition by Hydrocortisone
Relative Effectiveness of Stain-Removing
    Toothpaste
Are Human and Animal Blood Compatible?
Improving the Aerodynamic Efficiency of
    Human-Powered Vehicles
Computerized Transportation System for the
    Handicapped
Synthesis of Anticancer Drugs from Platinum
    Complexes

As you can see from this chapter, anything goes. Your project can be original or repetitive, investigative or nonexperimental, practical or theoretical, mathematical or musical, pictorial or written. No matter what format you choose, your project should be a pursuit of something that has aroused your curiosity and interest. In your pursuit, you will discover the spirit of science.

3
PLANNING FOR YOUR PROJECT

Before beginning work on your project, you must pay attention to some details that can save you work and time. These involve developing plans to refine your topic, locating sources of equipment and materials, and working out a time schedule for each phase of your project.

NARROW YOUR TOPIC

If you look again at some of the project titles listed on pages 23 and 24, you'll recall that some were too vague and gave you no idea where to begin. Once you have selected your topic and type of project, refine it so that you know exactly what you will be doing. This refining process is especially important if you plan to carry out an original investigation.

The library can be your best source for refining your proposal. Your detective skills will be important in tracking down and digging out the necessary information. Don't hesitate to ask the librarian for help. Even Holmes required Dr. Watson's assistance in solving some of his cases.

Although small in size, a local town pond might be too complex a subject to handle unless you refine your topic to a specific proposal.

Look for information that will help you get a better idea of what to do in your project. For example, if you developed an interest in acid rain from reading an article in a scientific journal, you should now refine this interest into a specific problem or question. Let's say you wanted to do a project with the title "What Are the Effects of Acid Rain on Town Pond?" You'll discover that a team of experts requiring several years of work and a considerable amount of money and equipment is likely needed to answer this question.

Town Pond is inhabited by numerous forms of plant and animal life, each composed of different age groups. These groups vary in biological activities, behavioral patterns, and seasonal adaptations.

Use the library to get more specific information about acid rain. You might come up with a plan to investigate the effects of acid rain on the photosynthetic rate of a specific plant or on the reproductive capacity of a particular animal found in Town Pond. A plan with either question is manageable and can yield some results within a reasonable time.

You do not have to work out all the details, but refine your topic only to get a specific statement about what you plan to do. Setting your proposal down on paper will help you focus on your plan and also allow others to offer suggestions and advice. You are not committed or limited to your proposal; you can change it as you work through the final plan for your project. As with any detective or scientific investigation, you can modify your proposal to accommodate unforeseen circumstances or problems.

RECORD WHAT YOU READ

While searching through the library, have index cards available for writing down important information. Organize the information on these cards. Each card should contain the author's name; the title, publisher, and date, for a book; the title, journal's name, volume, and pages, for a magazine article; and the title, name, volume, and pages, for an encyclopedia reference. Each card should also have a short summary of the main points covered in the book or article. Write down this information for every reference, even if you don't see how you might use it for your project. You may discover later that a reference you considered useless turns out to be quite helpful.

Arrange all your index cards in some logical or meaningful pattern. For example, if you are researching the area of antibiotics and bacteria, place all the cards with information on growing bacterial cultures into one group, those describing the various types of bacteria into another, any on the mechanism of antibiotic action into a third, and so on. At this point, set aside, but do not discard, any references that seem useless. Since you may find a time when you need a particular reference, save all your cards until your project is complete.

PLAN YOUR EQUIPMENT NEEDS

Next, plan what equipment, supplies, and materials you must have to conduct your project. A list of these items will help you organize everything you'll need. You can always change the list to add or delete items. Specify not only the types of items, but also their quantities.

Compare the equipment in the following two lists.

List 1

assorted glassware
incubator
growth media
bacterial cultures
antibiotics

List 2

100 150 x 15 mm glass petri dishes
100 20 x 150 mm Pyrex test tubes
1 culture incubator with 30 to 65 degrees Celsius
    range
50 grams of nutrient agar
2 cultures each of *E. coli*, *B. subtilis*, and *S. lutea*

1 kit of antibiotic disks containing penicillin,
erythromycin, neomycin, and streptomycin

List 1 is too vague; you have no idea what size the test tubes must be or how much agar will be needed to grow the bacteria. List 2 reflects a better plan, since it is more detailed and provides a clearer idea of the purpose of your project. You could easily locate all the items in a scientific supply company catalog. Knowing the type and quantity of each item, you can calculate the cost of purchasing it from a scientific supply company. Here are several companies you could use to order equipment and materials:

Carolina Biological Supply Co.
2700 York Rd.
Burlington, NC 27215

Central Scientific Co.
11222 Melrose Ave.
Franklin Park, IL 60131

Connecticut Valley Biological Supply Co.
82 Valley Road
Southampton, MA 01703

Edmund Science Co.
101 E. Goucester Pike
Barrington, NJ 08007

Fisher Scientific Co.
4901 W. LeMoyne Street
Chicago, IL 60651

Frey Scientific Co.
905 Hickory Lane
Mansfield, OH 44905

Learning Things, Inc.
PO Box 436
Arlington, MA 02174

Nasco
901 Janesville Ave.
Fort Atkinson, WI 53538

Sargent-Welch Scientific Co.
7300 N. Linder Ave.
Skokie, IL 60077

Science Kit and Boreal Labs
777 E. Park Drive
Tonawanda, NY 14150

Wards Natural Science Establishment
PO Box 1712
Rochester, NY 14603

Look through these catalogs to get ideas on what equipment and supplies are available for science projects. To avoid having to wait when you are ready to begin work, order the items once you have planned your list.

PLAN YOUR BUDGET

Determine the total cost for your equipment and materials. Don't despair if the amount is too high. There are a number of ways to cut down on your expenses. To begin, there's a good chance you can find most of what you need right in your school. Check to see what is available in the science, mathematics, and computer departments.

If your school doesn't have something you need, check local hospitals, medical offices, junk- and lumberyards, industrial sites, research facilities, or any other location where a donation may be obtained. Perhaps the cost for a temperature-controlled incubation chamber is too high. But a cabinet from the junkyard, a thermostat from a physics laboratory, insulation from a lumberyard, and spare parts from a hospital are just what you need to make that incubator.

Don't hesitate to ask people if they might have something to donate, so long as you explain the reason for your request. In most cases, they would prefer to see the item used rather than sitting in a storage closet waiting to be tossed. Be sure to write a thank-you note and acknowledge any contribution to your project.

Another good place to look for free materials is the industrial arts or shop class in your school. If your school offers classes in woodworking, small-engine repair, basic electronics, or similar subjects, your

Your school's industrial arts class may have
the tools, as well as the wood, metal, and
plastic, you need for your project.

industrial arts department is equipped with the machinery and tools to build something you may not be able to buy. With wood scraps and spare parts scattered around the shop, an industrial arts teacher may be the answer to your dilemma. Explain the reason for your request and provide the teacher with an adequate explanation of what you need. The teacher may even have some design improvements to suggest.

You can also get plans, ideas, and suggestions for building equipment from books (for example, *Teaching Science with Every Day Things*, *Scientific American Book of Projects for the Amateur Scientist*, and *Entertaining Science Experiments with Everyday Objects*), magazines specifically geared to science teaching (especially *The Science Teacher*, *Science and Children*, *The Journal of College Science Teaching*, and *The American Biology Teacher*), and publications aimed at the home hobbyist (including *Popular Mechanics* and *Home Mechanix*).

You might be able to substitute something for an item you cannot buy or locate, or just to save some money. Look around at what is available in school or at home and see if anything can be adapted to fit your needs. An assortment of jars can substitute for a supply of beakers, measuring cups for graduated cylinders, and an aquarium pump for an aerating system. Just check before anything goes into the garbage pail.

In fact, most science fair judges give credit for ingenuity and admire projects made possible because of creativity shown in overcoming an obstacle, perhaps a missing piece of equipment. A project showing some creativity may get more recognition than one in which the equipment was purchased. Judge for yourself by looking at how the following project reflected resourcefulness and creativity.

*If money for materials is a problem,
use substitutes: jars for beakers, cups
for graduated cylinders, and an aquarium
pump for an aerating system.*

ONE STUDENT'S SOLUTION
TO THE EQUIPMENT PROBLEM

John Lugbauer wanted to test the effects of slow air currents on different wing designs. He needed a rather sophisticated device to generate these air currents, measure their speed, and determine their effects on various types of wings. The cost of buying such a wind tunnel or having one built to his specifications was too high to be practical. Once John realized his problem, he set about looking for some alternatives.

His search led him to an attic fan, pieces of plywood, and scrap metal. The fan could obviously gen-

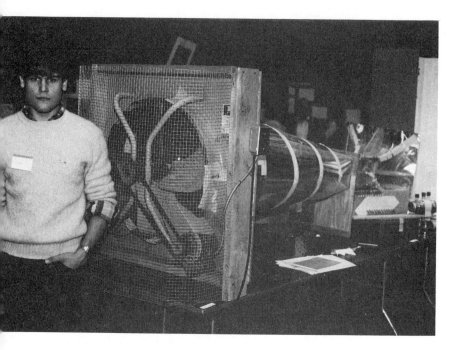

John Lugbauer depended on a donation, raffle, and his creativity to carry out his project.

erate air currents into a tunnel made from wood and metal. But a major problem was how to measure and record the airspeed produced by the attic fan. He found part of the answer by contacting a local aerospace research facility where John was able to borrow a specialized tube for measuring airspeeds.

John solved the rest of his problem by making the device for recording airspeeds from a mayonnaise jar from home, and glass tubing from school. Requiring some funds for buying materials to construct the wings, John participated in a raffle conducted by his school. The proceeds from the raffle tickets were divided among students engaged in science fair projects. With his share of the money, he was able to cut down on some of the expenses of buying the aluminum sheets, brass tubing, and Plexiglas needed to build the wings. John could then begin what was to become an award-winning project!

PLAN FOR SAFETY

In planning what you'll need, be aware of any equipment or materials that could be hazardous. Anything which could injure someone or pose a safety threat is always prohibited from a science fair competition. Projects are not allowed to display any disease-causing organisms, dangerous chemicals, combustible materials, explosive gases, open or concealed flames, radioactive sources, or any unsafe equipment. You can use these items only if they are necessary to carry out your project.

If you get permission to use such items, check with your teacher or a professional for information and safety precautions. Take the necessary safeguards to prevent any accidents. Many projects require some degree of caution if they require use of chemical reagents, open flames, or combustible materials. The only way to avoid these is to plan a project limited to a display of pictures and photographs or a written report based on library readings.

PLAN YOUR TIME

Finally, plan a time schedule. A model may require only a few hours of work to complete, while an original investigation may take hundreds of hours to finish. Be aware of the time required before you start your project. Talk to someone who has done a project, possibly similar to the one you're planning, and get an idea of how much time is involved.

Time (in days)		Date due
7	Selecting topic	October 15
15	Refining topic	November 15
5	Preparing plans	December 1
40	Conducting experiments	April 1
7	Evaluating results	April 15
10	Preparing report	May 1
1	Presenting project	May 15

Work out a schedule to help you make sure each phase of your project is finished on time. In this way you'll be sure to have your project ready to exhibit at the science fair.

Divide your project into small segments and set a due date for each one. In this way, you'll get a feeling of accomplishment as you meet the deadline for each step. For example, if you plan to build an original model, plan the dates for selecting your topic, refining your idea, gathering the equipment and materials, finishing the model, and preparing any written reports. If you plan to enter your model in a science fair, have everything ready by that date.

Once you have refined your topic, located sources to obtain equipment and materials, and worked out your time schedule, your plans are finished. Now get ready to begin the actual work.

4
THE SCIENTIFIC
METHOD

If you plan to do an original investigation for your project, you should be familiar with the approach scientists usually use in their experiments. This approach is known as the *scientific method*. The four basic steps of the scientific method include developing a purpose for your investigation, conducting experiments, recording the results, and reaching a conclusion. Obviously, if you have no organized method to conduct your investigation, you probably will get nowhere. On the other hand, if you do your investigations by following these four steps, you won't be guaranteed success, but you will be less likely to fail or give up hope of ever completing your project.

YOUR PURPOSE

For help in developing your proposal, first come up with a *hypothesis*. A hypothesis is nothing more than an educated guess, proposing a possible solution to the problem or question raised by your original investigation. Keep several factors in mind when forming your hypothesis.

First, base your hypothesis on the information you have gathered from your research, particularly library readings. You may have selected your topic after reading several articles in scientific journals. In this case, your hypothesis should take into account the results of any experiments or observations mentioned in these articles.

Second, your hypothesis should be clear and brief. It should provide a good idea of what you plan to do without being too wordy. State your hypothesis in one sentence: "Small amounts of caffeine will speed up the growth rate of earthworms." From reading just this one sentence, anyone can tell what you intend to explore in your investigation.

Third, you must be able to test your hypothesis. If you are planning to investigate whether caffeine speeds up the growth rate of earthworms, you can conduct experiments to test this hypothesis. You can place the earthworms in soil samples containing different amounts of caffeine and compare their growth rate to that of earthworms kept in soil without caffeine. However, you cannot form a hypothesis suggesting that caffeine will make the worms feel better, since you cannot perform any scientific tests to measure their feelings.

Once you have formed your hypothesis, prepare a brief statement explaining your purpose: "Caffeine is a drug that acts as a stimulant, speeding up many metabolic processes. The purpose of this project is to determine if caffeine will cause earthworms to grow at a faster rate."

Remember, your hypothesis is only an assumption or an educated guess. If you have read extensively to refine your topic, your hypothesis may be based on firmer ground, especially if you have a good deal of background information supporting your position. Nonetheless, your hypothesis is still only an educated guess. You may find the results of your investigation do not support and may even reject your hypothesis. Perhaps caffeine slows down the growth rate of earthworms.

Do not consider your project a failure if your investigation does not confirm your hypothesis. If this happens, *only* your hypothesis is discarded. The results of your investigation are still valid and can be used as part of your project. In fact, these results might be helpful in providing you with ideas and clues for future projects.

YOUR EXPERIMENTS

The next step of the scientific method is to design your experimental procedure. Outline the steps you will follow in attempting to reach some answer or conclusion about your hypothesis. Make the experimental design as simple as possible. The best scientific investigations are often simple in nature and direct in approach. The more complicated the design, the more chances for errors. In addition, you may never finish your project if it is too complex.

There are two types of experiments: qualitative and quantitative. A *qualitative* experiment can be conducted through careful observations without getting involved in measurements or statistical analysis. In a qualitative project, there may be no need to collect data by recording time, for example, or measuring changes in volumes.

A *quantitative* experiment involves measurements and collecting numerical data. If you plan to enter your original investigation in a science fair, be aware that the judges often look to see if you have included quantitative information wherever possible. Carefully

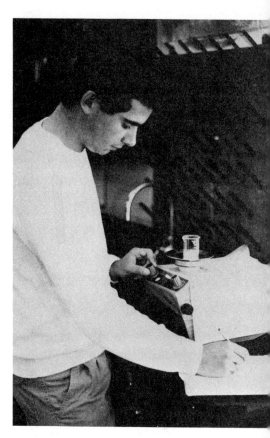

A quantitative experiment, unlike a qualitative one, involves measurements and the recording of data.

examine your experimental design to see where you can make some measurements and record numerical data. Although you may think your project does not require any measurements, a longer look may reveal some quantitative aspects.

For example, a project examining the food preferences of a particular invertebrate seems qualitative: the animal prefers lettuce to liver. Yet you should compile a data sheet, indicating the number of times the organisms responded to each type of food, how long each response took, and the length of time spent consuming the food.

Similarly, a project exploring the adaptations of insects to pesticides may not appear to be a quantitative investigation. You may simply observe whether the organisms live or die. However, you can measure and record the amount of pesticide used, the survival rate to various concentrations, and any abnormal growth patterns. You could then make a more specific or quantitative conclusion about the effects of the pesticide. Perhaps a particular concentration of pesticide is needed to produce an abnormality in growth.

THINK METRIC

All measurements in your quantitative investigation should be in metric units. Scientists throughout the world use the metric systrem to record length, volume, mass, and temperature. The English units of measurements are as precise, but they are more cumbersome to use when trying to convert from one unit to another.

The metric system is preferable because the units are based on multiples of 10, so converting from one unit to another is easy. Just move the decimal point a certain number of places to either the left or the right. For example, 6.2 millimeters equals 0.62 centimeter, and 0.024 kilogram equals 24 grams. In metric there is no need to divide by 12 as when converting inches to feet or to multiply by 16 as when changing pounds to ounces.

All your equipment and lab apparatus should be calibrated in metric. Do not use a cylinder or a thermometer graduated in English units with the idea of making all the conversions at the end of your investigation. The amount of time required to perform all the conversions might be discouraging. Use metric measurements from the start so that your frame of reference corresponds to the one used by scientists throughout the world. Even if you have had little or no experience with metric units, you'll find they are easy to use.

YOUR RESULTS

The third step in the scientific method is recording the results and data of your experiments. Appreciate the importance of data by heeding Holmes's warning as given to Dr. Watson: "I have no data yet. It is a capital mistake to theorize before one has data. Insensibly, one begins to twist facts to suit theories, instead of theories to suit facts." Like the great detective, you must collect sufficient data to explain the facts uncovered in your project.

Do not record the data on pieces of scrap paper or in an assortment of notebooks used for other purposes. Keep a notebook exclusively for your project data. You may want to take photographs or make drawings and diagrams of various stages of your experiments, especially if your project involves qualitative descriptions such as changes in color or patterns of behavior. In any case, do not attempt to commit results to memory; you'd be surprised how quickly any mental records of data will fade. Placing confidence in your ability to memorize will only cause you to lose data, some of which may be important pieces of the final solution.

YOUR CONCLUSION

With your data in hand, you have reached the last step of the scientific method: drawing a conclusion. Your data will either support or reject your hypothesis. Without a conclusion, your project will have failed to

Keep a notebook exclusively for recording any information, observations, and data about your project.

fulfill its purpose, since the whole reason for your investigation was to answer a question or solve a problem. Don't spend so much time carrying out your investigation that you rush through your data and fail to arrive at a conclusion. Science fair judges will be looking for a conclusion to any investigative project. Without a concluding statement, your project will be considered incomplete.

Your conclusion must come directly and solely from the data in your notebook. If you discover that you cannot arrive at any conclusion with your data, you may not have finished your experiments. You may have to perform more tests or check out some different approaches. Once you obtain a sufficient amount of data, make your conclusion. Be clear and concise. Don't hesitate to present *all* the conclusions your data can support. Do as much with the data as possible other than having it all neatly displayed, perhaps constructing charts or tables clearly showing your conclusions and interpretations.

On the other hand, don't reach any conclusion not justified by your data. If you claim something unsupported by the results of your investigation, others will discover this discrepancy when they examine your data. You must reach a balance when making conclusions, as much as possible but not more than justified. You can point out some possible findings of your investigation, but emphasize your results are only suggestive and not conclusive in these areas.

Again, don't worry if your data fail to support your hypothesis. You cannot change the data, but you can propose a different hypothesis and suggest a new set of experiments to test it. An insight into future possibilities would add to your credentials as a competent and thorough investigator.

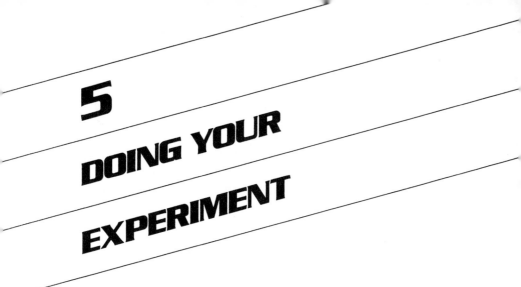

5
DOING YOUR EXPERIMENT

In following the scientific method, be aware of several factors scientists consider in designing and carrying out their experiments. Design your investigations so that you know what factor in the experiment is responsible for producing the results. In addition, collect accurate and sufficient data before making any conclusions. Finally, take precautions to reduce or eliminate sources of error wherever possible.

INCLUDE A CONTROL

An experiment often involves a *control*. A control sets up conditions in an experiment so that the investigator knows what factor is responsible for the results. Using a control is the only way to make sure that no more than one part of the problem or question is tested at a time.

Let's say you plan to investigate the effects of light intensity on the rate of photosynthesis in a freshwater plant. Your experimental design might involve submerging the plant in a test tube of fresh water and exposing it to light. When the light is turned on, the plant can photosynthesize.

Your hypothesis states that the greater the light intensity, the higher the rate of photosynthesis. From your biology course, you remember that a plant uses carbon dioxide and produces oxygen during photosynthesis. Your plan involves measuring the amount of oxygen produced by the plant as an indication of how much photosynthesis is occurring. The more oxygen produced, the higher the photosynthetic rate.

Your procedure involves varying the distance between the light source and the plant, and then measuring the amount of oxygen produced. Using several plants in different experiments over a period of three weeks, you discover that moving the light closer (up to a certain point) increases the photosynthetic rate. But can you be sure that the greater light intensity was responsible for the higher photosynthetic rate? Perhaps the rate increase was caused by the plant's being in better condition or having more carbon dioxide available for photosynthesis. The higher rate of photosynthesis may have also been due to the warmer temperature that day or the greater amount of water in the test tube.

In any case, you could not conclude that the greater light intensity was the factor responsible for the increased photosynthetic rate. If you included a control for this experiment, however, you could make a valid conclusion about the relationship between light intensity and the photosynthetic rate.

To establish a control, you need two experimental setups identical in all respects but one. In testing the effect of a particular light intensity on the photosynthetic rate, you would need two test tubes. One would have a plant submerged in water and exposed to light; the other would be the same, except placed in the dark. *All* other conditions would be the same: amount of water, size and shape of the plant, amount of carbon dioxide, and temperature.

The extent to which the light affected photosynthesis would be determined by subtracting the amount, if any, of oxygen produced by the plant placed in the dark from the amount produced by the plant exposed to light. Since all conditions except one are the same, you could prove a cause-and-effect relationship between the light source and the rate of photosynthesis: the greater light intensity must be the *only* factor responsible for any increase in the photosynthetic rate. With the use of a control for each experimental setup, you have eliminated all other possibilities.

THE NEED FOR A CONTROL

To be sure you understand how to establish a control, look over the following list. For each investigation, explain how you would set up the experiment.

The Effects of X Rays on Seed Germination
Evaluating the Effectiveness of Various Food
    Preservatives
Which Mouthwash Best Prevents Bacterial
    Growth?

In every case, you will need two groups identical in all respects but one. For example, divide the seeds into two groups: half are exposed to X rays, the other half are not. Treat one half of a food sample with a preservative; do not add any to the other half. Add a mouthwash to a bacterial culture; grow a culture of the same bacteria without the mouthwash. In each of these experiments, keep all other conditions between the two groups the same.

SOME IMPORTANT DEFINITIONS

You may come across some words or terms frequently used in investigative projects. Let's use the experiment testing the effects of different light intensities on the photosynthetic rate as an example. Any plants exposed to light make up the *experimental group*. The experimental group is the one exposed to the factor being tested, in this case light intensity. Those plants placed in the dark make up the *control group*. The control group is the one that is not exposed to the factor being tested in the experiment. In all other features, the experimental and control groups are identical.

The plan for this investigation calls for varying the light intensity; the experimenter is free to select any light intensity to observe what will happen. Since any light intensity can be used, this factor is called the *independent variable*. The independent variable is the factor that the experimenter is free to change at will, in this case the light intensity. The photosynthetic rate depends upon the light intensity and is known as the *dependent variable*. The dependent variable is the factor that the experimenter is causing to change, in this case the photosynthetic rate.

A control allows for only one independent variable to be tested at a time. Be careful to keep all other conditions the same. Whether unintentionally or accidentally, you must not favor the experimental group. Plants must be randomly divided between the experimental and control groups—don't select the "healthier-looking" plants for the experimental group. Also do not favor one group with more water, cleaner test tubes, or additional carbon dioxide. If you do, more than one independent variable would be present, and any conclusion you made would be invalid.

In some experimental designs, the independent variable can consist of two or more factors that the investigator simultaneously varies. For example, if you design an experiment to establish the optimum soil condition for growing tomato plants, one procedure might involve varying the amounts of sand, clay, and humus in each pot. One mixture might contain equal amounts of each ingredient, another mostly humus, a third mostly sand, and so on. In this experiment, the independent variable is the chemical composition of the soil. All other factors, such as water, temperature, and light, must be kept the same.

KEEP ACCURATE RECORDS

While doing your experiment, you will be collecting data. Record all your data in a notebook used only for your project. The format of your record book depends upon the nature of your investigation. The illustration on page 72 shows a form you could use for recording data from the experiments testing the effects of light intensity on photosynthesis.

Notice that the heading on the form contains spaces for the title of your project, the date, the number of times the independent variable was tested, and any additional information concerning the investigation. The columns are arranged so that the time elapsed and amount of oxygen produced can be easily recorded. Obviously, any format you design must include sufficient space for recording your test data. Set aside some additional space at the end of the form for general comments.

Include these comments as part of any record keeping, no matter what format you use for recording data. You may observe something unexpected, get an idea to check something else, or think of a way of improving your experimental design. In any case, have a place to jot down this information before you forget.

Title: Effect of Light Intensity on Photosynthesis   Date: 3/15/86
Distance: 30 cm.   Trial Number: 4
Comments:

Time (min.)	O₂ (ml.)	Comments

Prepare a form in your notebook so that you can record pertinent information, data, and any additional observations you may make.

Since you should carry out each experiment several times, make copies of your data form, using one for each experiment. No scientist can arrive at a valid conclusion from the results of one experiment. Before arriving at any conclusion, be sure to perform a sufficient number of tests.

For example, you may eventually test the effects of a light source placed at a certain distance ten times before reaching a valid conclusion. After all, if you recorded 6 milliliters of oxygen produced the first time, and 20 milliliters the second, then you would be premature in concluding that 13 milliliters (the average of the two results) represented the amount produced at that distance. However, if you performed ten trials and obtained measurements of 6, 20, 17, 9, 14, 10, 16, 12, 18, and 8 milliliters, then your average of 13 milliliters would be based on more substantial data.

OBJECTIVITY IS THE RULE

Be objective and do not allow your personal feelings or opinions to interfere with your experiments. You may observe a result totally out of agreement with other data. Do not discard this result—there are no incorrect answers when conducting an experiment, only unexpected ones!

Although some results may not be understandable at the time, analyzing your records at a later date may reveal a possible explanation. Perhaps the lone result was caused by contaminated glassware, faulty equipment, or a math error. Even if your records do not provide any immediate explanation, an unexpected result may not be an error but a clue to some interesting discovery or accidental finding. Don't forget—penicillin was discovered when Fleming made an unexpected observation while working with bacterial cultures.

Any accidental finding points out that the scientific method is only a guideline for conducting an investigative project. Don't be afraid to branch out from your work or follow tangents suggested by your data. Obviously you cannot be trained to make an accidental discovery, but you can remain alert to ideas, clues, suggestions, and leads provided by your data. Not following up an interesting development may save some time. After all, the science fair might be rapidly approaching, and your project has to be completed on time. But what if that one unexpected result were to lead to an interesting finding or an important discovery?

EXPERIMENTS ARE NOT
FREE FROM ERROR

Errors can occur in any experiment, as a result of faulty instrumentation, imprecise measurements, human mistakes, or other reasons. However, these types of errors cannot detract from the quality of a good project. Don't hesitate to admit your mistakes, but instead follow the example of Lara Ausubel. Lara explored the mechanism of action of Verapamil, a drug used in the treatment of coronary artery disease.

Lara had read medical reports indicating that this drug probably prevented heart spasms by inhibiting the action of nerves that cause the smooth muscle of the heart to contract. She also learned that Verapamil blocks the flow of calcium ions across the membranes of nerve cells and also slows down the cilia of cells lining the trachea, or windpipe, of rats. She got the idea of investigating whether Verapamil acted directly on heart cells rather than through controlling nerves.

Lara used single-celled organisms known as protozoans. These organisms have cilia but no nerves, allowing her to test if the drug directly affected the cilia. She added serial dilutions of the drug to measured volumes of the protozoans (see the table on page 75). Lara set up appropriate controls and repeated each experiment several times. She observed the effects of the drug by making microscopic observations.

Lara observed that as the concentration of Verapamil increased, all the cilia became paralyzed, suggesting the drug worked directly on the heart cells rather than on the nerves that control it. She also discovered that this paralysis was caused by the drug blocking the conversion of a chemical known as ATP into another compound known as cAMP.

Table 12. The Assay of cAMP in spring water and in *Paramecium* cultures, untreated versus treated with various concentrations of *Isoptin* ®, using the method of Tovey as modified by Chiang*

	cAMP levels in picomoles/ml.		
	Run 1	Run 2	Average
Spring water	0.00	0.00	0.00
Untreated Paramecia diluted with spring water (1:1)	0.17	0.23	0.20
Paramecia treated with *Isoptin* ® 1:750 (1:1)	0.17	0.28	0.22
Paramecia treated with *Isoptin* ® 1:700 (1:1)	0.09	0.27	0.18
Paramecia treated with *Isoptin* ® 1:600 (1:1)	0.20	0.17	0.19
Paramecia treated with *Isoptin* ® 1:500 (1:1)	0.10	0.21	0.16
Paramecia treated with *Isoptin* ® 1:500 (1:1)	—**	0.16	0.16
Paramecia treated with *Isoptin* ® 1:400 (1:1)	0.13	0.10	0.12
Paramecia treated with *Isoptin* ® 1:300 (1:1)	0.10	0.08	0.09
Paramecia treated with *Isoptin* ® 1:200 (1:1)	0.06	0.18	0.12
Paramecia treated with *Isoptin* ® 1:100 (1:1)	0.00	0.06	0.03
Paramecia treated with *Isoptin* ® 1:50 (1:1)	0.00	0.00	0.00
Paramecia treated with *Isoptin* ® 1:10 (1:1)	0.00	0.00	0.00
Paramecia treated with *Isoptin* ® 1:5 (1:1)	0.00	0.00	0.00
Paramecia treated with *Isoptin* ® 1:2 (1:1)	0.00	0.00	0.00
Paramecia treated with *Isoptin* ® (1:1)	0.00	0.00	0.00

* [^{3}H] Cyclic AMP Assay kit supplied by Diagnostic Products Corporation, Los Angeles, California

** Some of the ^{3}H cAMP was spilled during transfer, making analysis impossible

Again check the illustration for the culture treated with the 1:500 dilution. Notice that Lara could not report any results for run 1 since some of the cAMP was spilled during the transfer—a human error. However, this in no way affected the outcome of her project.

Lara received highest honors at the regional science fair and was selected to enter the state competition, where she again won highest honors and received first prize for best biology project. The judges obviously recognized the scientific value of her project and totally ignored the minor mistake in one of her experiments.

HOW TO CONTROL
SOME ERRORS

You cannot completely eliminate errors, but you can control them. If a piece of equipment gives erratic readings, try to get it repaired or replaced. However, nothing can be done about the slight, built-in variations in certain lab apparatus such as balances, thermometers, and rulers, or about minor, human misjudgment when measuring. Weigh the same object on ten different balances to the nearest 0.01 gram, and you may not get the same measurement in all cases. Record the temperature of a water bath with ten different thermometers, and you may find slight differences.

Be careful not to alow errors to get out of hand to the point where they invalidate your data. The accuracy of your data depends on how precise and careful you are when making measurements. The more accurate your data, the more solid your basis for making conclusions. Being precise and accurate in collecting data will also reflect your credentials as a competent investigator.

6 PREPARING YOUR REPORT

No matter what type of project you do, you will have to prepare a report summarizing your work. If your project centers around a model, pictorial display, or a repetition of someone else's work, your report will probably be less extensive than one describing an original investigation. Still, you can use your imagination to make your report interesting, perhaps even extraordinary.

For example, if you build a model, include drawings or plans showing the various stages of construction. A blueprint drawn to scale of the completed model can be a way of including some quantitative data into your report. You can explain technical problems encountered or scientific applications uncovered while assembling the model.

For a project centering on a pictorial display, your report can describe the scientific story behind the photographs, pictures, or drawings. If your project involves a repetition of a classic experiment, include suggestions for improvement or ideas for additional investigations.

If you have conducted a thorough and extensive lab investigation, you may face a problem shared by Dr. Watson, who wrote, "When I glance over my notes and records of the Sherlock Holmes cases ... I am faced by so many which present strange and interesting features that it is no easy matter to know which to choose and which to leave." Your notebook containing data may be filled like Dr. Watson's chronicles. Where do you begin and what will you choose to include in your report?

WHAT TO INCLUDE IN YOUR REPORT

Start by preparing a cover or title page for your report. Don't underestimate the importance of a good title. Spend some time thinking about the title. A good one will grab everyone's attention. Don't be vague; if possible include both the independent and dependent variables tested in your investigation. Consider the following two titles:

A Burning Issue—
    The Effects of Retardants on Flammability
Computer Math

The first title is not only creative but also gives an idea about what the project covers. The second title provides little information other than that the project involves computers and math.

THE BODY OF YOUR REPORT

There are no absolute rules as to how you should write your report, but most papers are prepared according to the format used in scientific journals: brief summary of the work; introduction; explanation

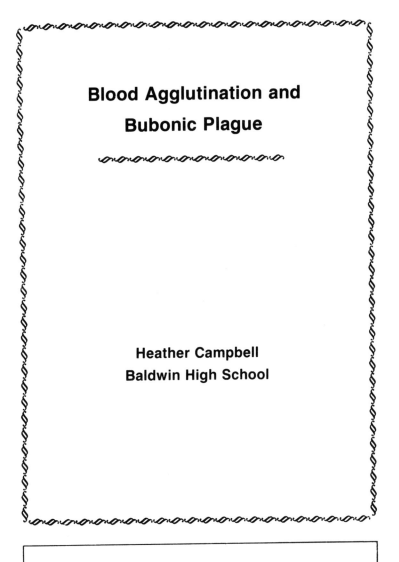

Blood Agglutination and
Bubonic Plague

Heather Campbell
Baldwin High School

Include the title of your project, your name, and
the name of your school on the title page of your
report. Type or use Prestype for a neat and
legible appearance.

of the methods; results; conclusions, including the significance of the work; and bibliography. Although you can write your report in longhand, it will be more impressive and easier to read if you type it—or word-process and print it—double-spaced with one-inch margins on 8½-by-11-inch paper.

A brief summary of a written scientific report is called an *abstract*. Although the abstract comes first, you may find it easier to write it after you have finished your entire report. Since your abstract is probably the only part of your report the science fair judges will read carefully, be clear and concise. Explain the purpose, procedure, and conclusion of your project in three or four paragraphs totaling between 200 and 250 words. Choose your words carefully, since you want to arouse the reader's interest in your project. See how the following abstract accomplishes these objectives.

The purpose of my project is to explore the virulence relationships among three species of the bacterial genus *Yersiniae*. The best-known species is an intracellular parasite responsible for bubonic plague. The other two are less virulent but can cause severe gastrointestinal disease in humans and animals.

Research work indicates that the virulence of these species depends on genes located on the plasmids, pieces of hereditary material separate from the main bacterial chromosome. Little is known, however, about the role of these plasmid genes in causing disease.

These plasmids also produce a substance which agglutinates red blood cells. Since the production of this substance can be observed and quantitatively read, a study of this blood clotting process could serve as a model for understanding how these bacteria cause disease.

Significant variations of the blood-clotting substance were found among the three species, with the highest level present in the species responsible for bubonic plague. Perhaps the ability to cause rapid and severe clumping of blood and the subsequent clogging of capillaries accounts for the increased virulence of this one species.

This abstract was part of a written report submitted by Heather Campbell. Heather must have aroused your interest in the first paragraph by mentioning bubonic plague. She continued in the second paragraph to give a little of the background information which provided the idea for her project. The last two paragraphs include a summary of her methods, results, and conclusion.

STATE YOUR PURPOSE

The next section of your report is a brief introduction, explaining the general nature of your project. State what the project attempted to prove and what independent and dependent variables you tested. If you check your hypothesis, you'll probably discover that a simple rewording with a few additional remarks are all you need to write your introduction.

The introduction should also include the relevant background information about your topic. Refer to the notes you wrote on index cards to refine your topic. Use any information that establishes the importance of your investigation. Review the significant literature in your own words, referring to a variety of sources (books, periodicals, pamphlets, encyclopedias, etc.), and cite the references in a bibliography.

Be brief: all you want to accomplish is to familiarize the reader with similar research work that laid the groundwork for your project. After discussing the purpose of your investigation, explain what impact your investigation might have on scientific knowledge or technological know-how.

EXPLAIN YOUR METHODS

Now that you have filled your reader with interest and curiosity about your project, explain how you carried out your investigation. You must carefully detail the exact process followed so that anyone can repeat your experiment just from reading the description in your report. Provide a complete list of equipment, materials, chemicals, specimens, and apparatus. Thoroughly describe all the steps and give complete instructions for building any equipment.

Imagine if you bought an unassembled bicycle, only to discover that all the parts were included but that the assembly instructions were missing. Even if the instructions were provided, you could not assemble the bike correctly if they were incomplete or had the steps out of sequence. You may want to include photographs or diagrams to illustrate complex points or sophisticated equipment. Even if you do not understand the terms and abbreviations in the following description, read it anyway to see how specific Heather was in describing her procedure for growing and collecting bacterial cells.

Bacteria were inoculated at 26° C for 24 hours. Organisms were washed in 0.033 M potassium phosphate buffer (pH 7.0) and inoculated into the defined liquid medium of Higuchi as modified by Zahorchak (Carter, P. B., et al., 1980, p. 638) at an optical density (O.D.$_{260}$) of 0.1. Cells were incubated on a waterbath shaker at 26° C in Erlenmeyer flasks (10 ml/125 ml flask) until late log phase for two transfers. Final transfers were to the same media at an O.D.$_{620}$ of 0.1.

Any pH adjustment was made at the final transfer. After incubation until late log phase, cells were spun down in the centrifuge (Sorvall RC2-B) at 10,000 rpm (12,000 g) for 20 minutes. The supernatant was poured off and bacterial cells were resuspended in phosphate buffer to a density of 4×10^{10} CFU/ml.

Heather's method for growing and collecting bacterial cells is detailed enough so that anyone could repeat her procedure from her report. She even provided a reference listed in her bibliography for anyone wishing to check the original paper for preparing the liquid medium.

This procedure provided Heather with the high concentrations of bacteria she needed in order to study how these organisms might be responsible for bubonic plague. You don't have to work with disease-causing bacteria, but every step of your procedure must be explained in as much detail as Heather's.

FOLLOW UP WITH RESULTS

The next section of your report should contain the results. In addition to a straightforward display of the data in rows and columns, use graphs and diagrams. Remember that your report should be comprehensive. Include any failures, errors, or results you can't explain. Don't analyze or interpret your data in this section; simply report the results in a clear and organized manner. You may have to spend time looking through your record book to group results from similar experiments.

CONCLUDE YOUR REPORT

After you have organized your results, the time has come for explaining, interpreting, and evaluating your data. Carefully examine your data to determine what they indicate. Is your hypothesis supported or rejected? Don't hesitate in being direct when concluding that the data did not verify your hypothesis. Remember that failure to obtain supporting evidence does not mean the project is a failure.

Don't limit concluding remarks to an explanation of your results. Perhaps your findings have application in other areas. For example, a study of factors affecting the friction produced between certain materials may have some application in designing cars. Suggest possible experiments to determine whether some application exists.

Also, don't hesitate to recommend changes or improvements that can be made in your project. Any ideas to extend the project would show your interest to improve your investigative skills. To show how you can follow up on a clue, suggest possibilities for future experiments based on leads provided by your data. Be careful not to confuse conclusions with suggestions. Base any conclusion on analysis of your data, and any suggestion on extension of your data.

INCLUDE YOUR REFERENCES

The last section of your report should be a list of all your references in the form of a bibliography. A bibliography contains all the books, encyclopedias, pamphlets, and periodicals that you used in researching your topic. Organize this list in alphabetical order.

The following forms are generally used in citing a reference: for a book—last name of author, first name, title, city of publication, publisher, date of publication; for an article—last name of author, first name, title of article, name of journal, volume number, pages. Accuracy is important, since you want to give proper credit to any scientist whose work provided the basis for your project. Check the bibliography at the end of this book, not only to see how to prepare one but also to locate other references that might help you with your project.

Acknowledge anyone who provided advice and suggestions in a section that follows your bibliography. Also include people who donated materials, allowed use of their facilities, or helped with the construction of equipment. As part of your written report, include any forms that have been signed by a teacher or professional, verifying that you have followed the recommended guidelines in using hazardous materials, vertebrate animals, or human subjects.

SCIENTIFIC WRITING: CONTENT

Use the following checklist to see if your report answers all the following questions:

1. What problem or question is being investigated?
2. What background information exists on this topic?
3. What equipment and materials were used in your experiment?
4. What procedures were followed to solve the problem or answer the question in this project?
5. What observations were made during the course of the investigation?
6. What information and data were recorded?
7. What conclusions were made regarding the original problem or question?
8. What suggestions were included for further research work to solve the problem more convincingly or answer the question more thoroughly?

9. What new problems or questions were uncovered by the project?
10. What sources were used?

SCIENTIFIC WRITING: STYLE

Make your report clear, simple, and accurate so that everybody can understand your work. Don't assume that someone reading your report is scientifically well versed; no one can be knowledgeable about all areas or disciplines of science. Although not everyone might appreciate the full significance of your investigation, they should have a clear understanding of its general nature and significance.

Clarity is the direct outcome of simplicity. Every word in a scientific paper should have a purpose. Don't use more words than necessary. You may think that the longer the report, the more impressed your readers will be. Consider, however, that the readers you must impress are the science fair judges. Impress them with quality, not quantity.

To improve the quality, begin by realizing that you're not finished after the report has been written— it's only the first draft. Go over your paper several times to see how words can be eliminated, sentences made simpler, or paragraphs clarified. Your written report is the *only* way everyone can appreciate what you've accomplished, so give it as much thought, enthusiasm, and effort as you devoted to conducting your project. Be especially alert to points considered serious faults in any scientific report.

Don't be whimsical in presenting data. Information presented in a disorganized manner reflects uncertainty and may require more time for interpretation than your reader is willing to spend. Check for organization and continuity in your report. Be sure that the content within each paragraph is interrelated. Use transitional sentences to connect sections.

Be totally objective—don't exclude data that conflict with your position. As a scientist, you must not exhibit prejudice in drawing any conclusions; your report must clearly show the steps you took in analyzing your data to reach a conclusion.

The need for accuracy is self-explanatory. A scientific report implies content based on recorded observation and documented evidence. You want the readers not only to understand what you did but also to agree with your conclusions. Your report should convince your readers that your interpretation of the data is the only possible explanation.

To determine if your report satisfies the content of scientific writing, ask your science teacher to read it. To check its style, grammar, punctuation, and spelling, ask your English teacher to read it. After these teachers read your report, you may have to rewrite it. You may find the rewriting tedious, but you will discover that the result is worth the effort. If you use word processing on a microcomputer to prepare your report, any rewriting will be much easier.

If your project wins an award at the fair, check with your science teacher for suggestions as to which journals might be interested in publishing your report. Even if your report does not appear in a scientific journal, most fairs publish the abstracts of the winners. Your written report can also be featured in your school's newspaper or newsletter, highlighting events in the science department. Not only will your published report reflect your hard work and enthusiasm, but it will also serve as inspiration for others who are planning to do a science fair project.

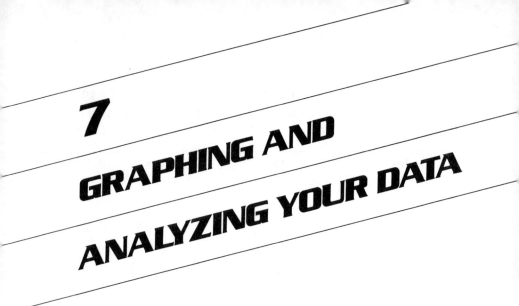

7

GRAPHING AND ANALYZING YOUR DATA

Simply displaying your data may not be the most effective way to show what your project accomplished. Rather than placing your data in columns and rows, use a graph or chart to show a clearer relationship between the variables. There are three common types of graphs: line, bar, and pie.

The one to use depends upon the nature of your investigation. If you tested the effects of an independent variable, use a line graph. If you analyzed the relative effectiveness of several products, present your data with a bar graph. If you conducted a survey, display your results with a pie chart. You can display your data in all three ways and then decide which is best. By the way, there's no reason why you can't design an entirely different format if you're not satisfied with any one of these.

LINE GRAPHS

Several different kinds of paper are available for making line graphs, each with a specific purpose. Select

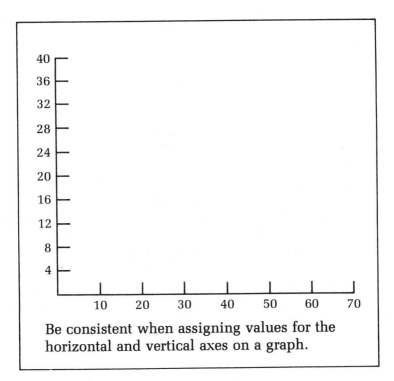

Be consistent when assigning values for the horizontal and vertical axes on a graph.

the one best suited to your needs. You may have to experiment with different ones before deciding, or you can check with your math teacher for advice. No matter which type of graph paper you will be using, be sure that you follow the correct procedures for plotting data.

Always place the dependent variable on the vertical axis and the independent variable on the horizontal axis. Next plot your points as accurately as possible. Be consistent when assigning your values for the vertical and horizontal axes. Let's say you decide to have each division on the vertical axis represent 10 milliliters, while each division on the horizontal axis represents 5 grams. Once you have decided the value for each division, you cannot arbitrarily vary the scale. For example, you cannot change a division on the vertical axis to represent a 5-milliliter increase.

Draw the graph to fill the paper as much as possible, rather than squeezing all the points into a small section. By using the whole graph, you can convey a clearer picture of any slight, but important, difference between two points.

When plotting the results of several experiments on the same graph, use symbols to distinguish between the curves. Provide an explanation at the bottom of the graph showing what each symbol represents. In place of symbols, you may want to label each curve on the graph or use a different color for plotting the results from each experiment.

BAR GRAPHS

Construct a bar graph by drawing a rectangular box from a point on the vertical axis down to the horizontal axis. As with a line graph, place the dependent variable along the vertical axis and the independent variable along the horizontal axis. Again be consistent when constructing the scale along each axis. In cases where you record several experiments on one graph, distinguish the bars for a particular investigation by using diagonal lines.

PIE CHARTS

A pie chart is another way to graph your data. A pie chart consists of a circle divided into pieces. Pie charts are commonly used to show the results of a survey. The whole pie represents the total number of people interviewed, while each piece stands for the proportional size of one of the groups in the survey. The size

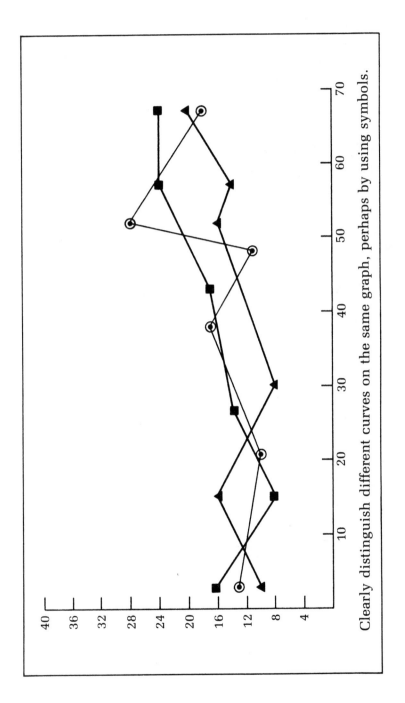

Clearly distinguish different curves on the same graph, perhaps by using symbols.

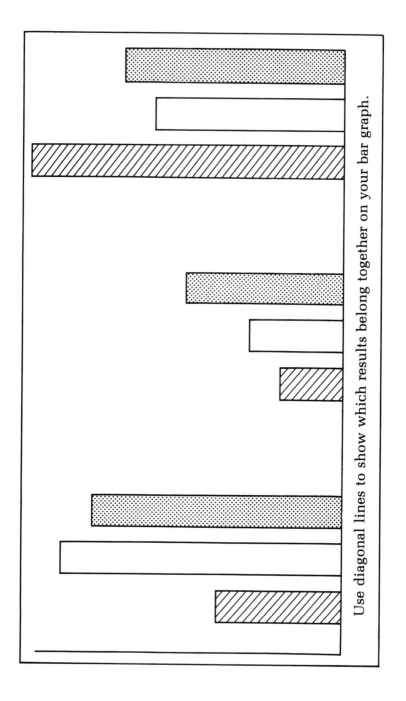

Use diagonal lines to show which results belong together on your bar graph.

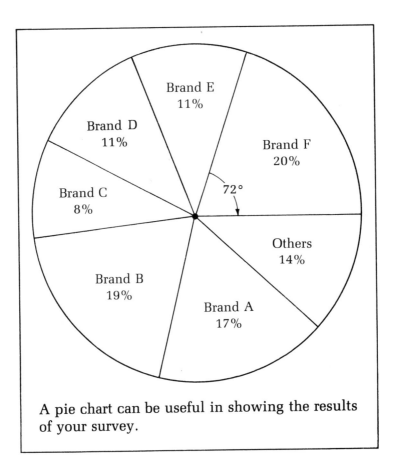

A pie chart can be useful in showing the results of your survey.

of each piece is calculated by determining the percent for a particular category and multiplying that number by 360 degrees (the total for the circle).

For example, if 20 percent of the population favored a particular soft drink, multiply 0.20 by 360 degrees to obtain 72 degrees. Using a protractor, draw a section with an angle of 72 degrees. Divide the rest of the circle in a similar manner. Pool any results where the numbers are too small, and label this section as "others."

ANALYZING YOUR RESULTS

Your results are significant only if you can arrive at a specific conclusion. Spending a considerable amount of time in carrying out experiments only to find your results are inconclusive can be quite disheartening. For example, if you tested a chemical for its effectiveness in stopping cells from dividing, you want to be sure your results are due to the action of the drug and not the result of chance. A statistical analysis can indicate if your results are meaningful: is there a significant difference between your experimental group (cells exposed to the drug) and control group (cells not exposed to the drug)?

Although such a statistical analysis may sound complicated, the calculations are quite simple. In fact, anytime you determine an average, you are performing a statistical analysis. An average or an arithmetic mean can help you decide whether a significant difference exists between the experimental and control groups.

The median is another statistically derived number, representing the middle measurement. There are equal numbers of measurements above and below the median. The median can help you get some insight into the distribution of results. Two different experiments may have the same average result, but the median can reveal some interesting differences.

Other statistical tests include determining the standard deviation, standard error of the mean, goodness-of-fit (chi square test), and linear correlation. The calculations used for each of these procedures are beyond the scope of this book.

However, you can see how to do these analyses by referring to an introductory text such as *Statistics for Biologists* or *Basic Statistical Techniques for Engineering & Science Students.*

If you work with computers, you may want to write a program that analyzes and graphs your data. Such a program can be an impressive part of your report. Whether you analyze by calculator or computer, just be sure you know enough about the simple kinds of statistical analyses, especially if you are working with a large amount of data. Only then can you reach a valid conclusion.

8
PREPARING YOUR PROJECT FOR EXHIBIT

When your project is finished, the time has come to prepare it for presentation at a science fair. You must prepare an exhibit, summarizing what you have accomplished in your project. Since you will not be able to include everything in your exhibit, you will have to be selective. Carefully choose what you will include, especially anything original, unusual, or creative. Plan your exhibit to attract everyone's attention by selecting interesting highlights and impressive illustrations.

BUILDING YOUR EXHIBIT

Science fairs often feature such a large number of projects that regulations usually limit the dimensions of each exhibit to 30 inches (76 centimeters) from front to back, 48 inches (122 centimeters) from side to side, and 48 inches (122 centimeters) higher than the table. Most exhibits follow a basic format: three panels that are self-supporting so that they rest on a table. This three-sided arrangement is only a suggested

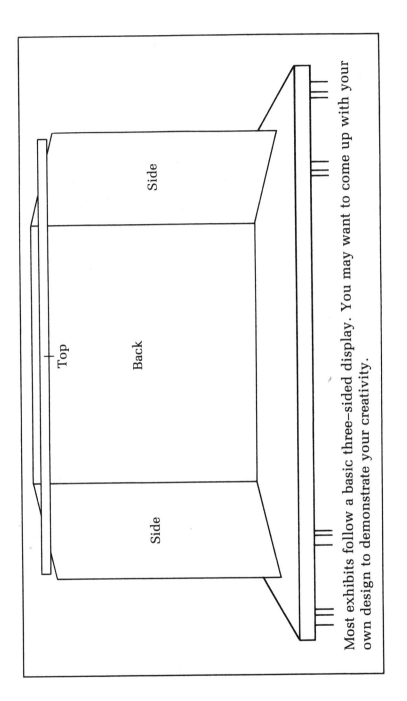

Most exhibits follow a basic three-sided display. You may want to come up with your own design to demonstrate your creativity.

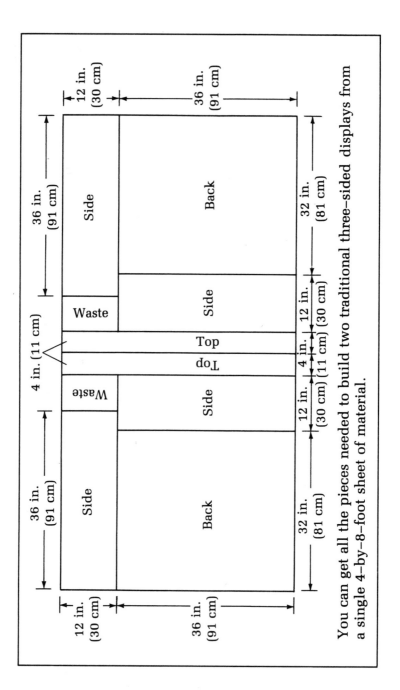

You can get all the pieces needed to build two traditional three–sided displays from a single 4–by–8–foot sheet of material.

format. Stand out from the crowd by coming up with your own design, perhaps using a different geometric pattern for the panels.

Whether you choose the traditional or an original format, use only sturdy materials such as plywood, masonite, homasote, pegboard, or heavy cardboard. You can obtain all the pieces needed to build two traditional three-sided exhibits from a single piece of 4-by-8-foot sheet. Paint or cover the material with colored paper to avoid an unfinished or rough appearance. Hinge the three panels together to make setting up and breaking down the exhibit much easier.

Before constructing the exhibit, make a sketch drawn to scale to help you plan where to place all the items on the panels. Be as detailed as possible, indicating exact sizes, shapes, and positions. Assemble a mock-up out of cardboard to help you decide where to position the items. Generally, most exhibits follow a basic arrangement, but you can use your imagination to create your own arrangement.

The center panel usually displays the title of the project and several diagrams, drawings, and illustrations. The left panel often contains information about the purpose and procedures of the project, while the right panel displays the results and conclusions.

The lettering for any titles on your panels should be neat, plain, and readable from a distance of 2 meters. You can cut the letters from colored construction paper and attach them to the panels with rubber cement, glue, or tape. Apply as little adhesive as possible to avoid wrinkling the letters. Do not use staples, since they would be visible and detract from the appearance of your lettering.

You can also draw the titles with stencils and then color them, or use stick-on letters known as Prestype, available from office supply stores. Prestype comes in a sheet, containing letters, numbers, and symbols.

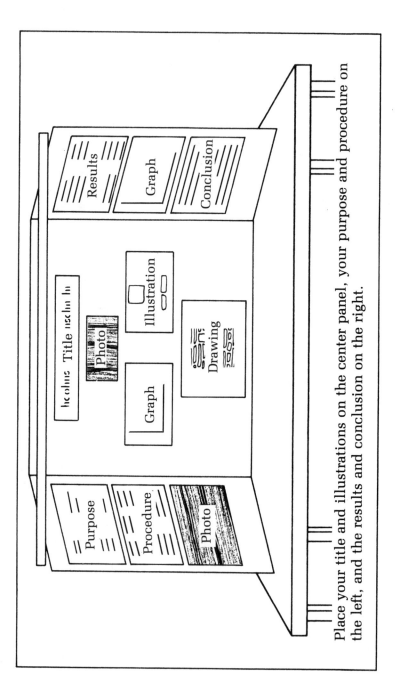

Place your title and illustrations on the center panel, your purpose and procedure on the left, and the results and conclusion on the right.

These are available in several different sizes. To transfer the Prestype to your display, place it over the paper or cardboard and then rub gently with a pencil or blunt-pointed object.

Carefully check your spelling, not only in your titles but in everything in your exhibit. Neatly draw your graphs and charts. Type your text material rather than writing it. Nothing may give a worse first impression than a misspelled word, a sloppy graph, or illegible writing. You may have to overcome a negative opinion of your project even before you've had a chance to talk about your work.

EXHIBIT PHOTOGRAPHS
AND DRAWINGS

If you have a camera or a cooperative friend, take photographs recording the progress of your project. These photographs would be the only way to display any large equipment or research facilities you used to conduct your investigation. You can also display photographs of your model at various stages of construction, people used in your survey, or any specimens too large to include in your exhibit.

Use 5-by-7-inch or 8-by-10-inch black-and-white or color photographs; smaller pictures won't show important details. Color is preferable to black-and-white for attracting someone's eye. However, black-and-white photographs can be quite striking provided the contrast is good. Don't staple or glue the photographs to your panels; mount them on cardboard to enhance their appearance. Get additional advice from someone at your local photo shop for suggestions on how to take and display photographs.

In preparing any drawings or charts, avoid materials that smudge: chalk, pastels, crayons, charcoal, etc. While handling your exhibit, you may accidentally

Louis Paul, a finalist in the national
Westinghouse Science Talent Search

smear the illustrations. If you must use anything that
might smudge, keep it covered with clear acetate until
the last possible moment.

Don't mount your photographs and drawings in an
arbitrary fashion, but try to organize them in some
eye-catching arrangement. Select the most important
visuals from your project. Some displays lose their
appeal because too much is included and the highlights of the project get lost in the confusion. Also,
avoid too much color or gaudy combinations, since
they will detract from the visual appeal of your exhibit.

Since you want your display seen in the best possible light, bring one or two portable lamps from home. You may find that lighting conditions in the exhibition hall are poor, making your display difficult to see and impossible to read. If there is an electrical outlet near your table, use the lamps to illuminate your display, positioning the lights to obtain the best effect. Make sure that the lights do not distract from your display by producing a bright glare.

WHAT ELSE TO EXHIBIT

If you exhibit a model, it should be neat, with sanded surfaces and polished parts. Use paints to make your model as attractive as possible. Make sure your model

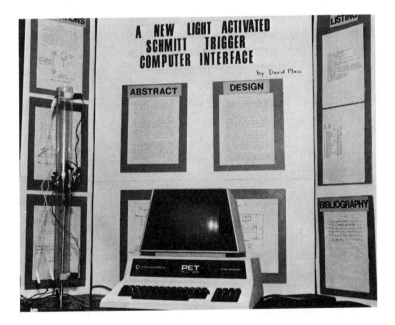

A science fair project by David Plass

doesn't fall to the ground in all the confusion of setting up your exhibit. Attach it to a plywood base if necessary. Include any diagrams, photographs, and especially information you have learned as a result of constructing your model.

For a display project, exhibit samples of the most interesting and unusual specimens in your collection. If you cannot include them because they are too large or dangerous, use photographs. Also exhibit some written material, explaining the scientific knowledge you've gained from your display project.

Any exhibit of a survey project will probably contain more written material than one for a model or display. But if you include only written material, your exhibit may not look too appealing or interesting. Display some relevant illustrations, colorful graphs, or informative charts. Add any small touch that will improve the appearance of your exhibit: place your written information on a color background, enclose the questionnaire used in your survey in a plastic binder, or include some photographs of the people you contacted.

If you did a project involving lab work, place your complete report, materials used in the investigation, or samples from your experimental group on the table in front of the exhibit. In that way, the backboard, side panels, and table comprise a comprehensive exhibit of your project.

WHAT TO EXCLUDE
FROM YOUR EXHIBIT

Exclude items that add little information about your project. A large number of items on display does not mean your project is more comprehensive or detailed. Too many items may detract from the important points of your exhibit. Start with materials that convey the most information. You can use the other materials if you have some space to fill.

You may not be allowed to exhibit anything considered hazardous to the public, including disease-causing organisms, microbial cultures, food materials, dangerous chemicals, combustible gases, flames, gas tanks, glassware such as syringes and pipettes, and certain types of lasers.

Any exhibits involving an operating device may be subject to certain restrictions, including the prohibition of high-voltage equipment, batteries with open-top cells, bare wiring, and temperatures exceeding 100 degrees Celsius. All electrical wiring must be properly insulated, and all switches located out of the reach of any observer. Science fair officials have the right to remove any exhibit that is considered hazardous or potentially dangerous, so be sure to check the rules and regulations before you arrive at the fair.

There's another important thing to do before you take your exhibit to the fair: prepare your presentation to explain the nature of your project. Consider your presentation as important as any other part of your project.

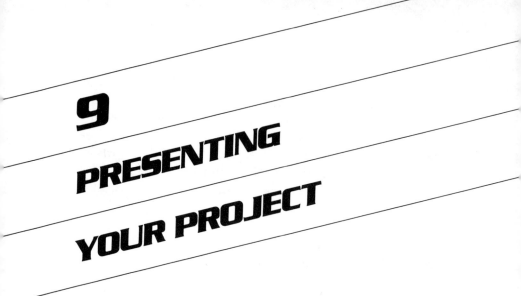

9
PRESENTING YOUR PROJECT

Don't wait until the day of the fair to begin preparing your talk for the science fair judges. Not only will you be busy making last-minute preparations on your display, but you will also find the exhibit hall too noisy and confusing to think. All the participants will be scampering about looking for their assigned spaces and hauling their projects into the hall.

PRACTICE MAKES PERFECT

Plan what you will say to the judges well in advance of the fair. Rehearsing your talk with your parents, teachers, and friends is an excellent way to practice before the real thing. Listen to a tape recording of your presentation to hear how it sounds to others. If you are not satisfied, make changes and then repeat the process. The more you practice, even in front of a mirror, the greater your chances of impressing your listeners. You may have as little as five minutes and certainly no more than ten to present your project, so effective communication is necessary.

Since eye contact with the judges is important to keep their attention, you should not read your presentation from note cards. You can refer to an outline to guide you through the presentation, but don't read the report word-for-word or repeat it from memory. If you do, you are likely to deliver your presentation in a monotone voice. The judges might find your presentation boring. In addition, you're more likely to get flustered if a judge interrupts you to ask a question. Deliver your speech with spontaneity and enthusiasm. Project your voice so that all the judges can hear.

HOW TO LOOK AND ACT

Since the judges will be looking at you during the presentation, don't chew gum, wear old or dirty clothes, sway back and forth, or peer into the distance. People are impressed with good manners, appropriate dress, polite behavior, and an interested attitude. Even though your behavior has nothing to do with the merits of your project, the judges might get a negative impression from your appearance that carries over into their evaluation of your project. Just think about a time when you may have formed a negative opinion of someone solely on the basis of his or her appearance.

Be sure not to block the judges' view by standing in front of your project; place yourself to the side so that they can clearly see your exhibit. Get them actively involved by giving them a copy of your abstract or arouse their interest by handing them a live specimen. To maintain their interest, make periodic eye contact with each of the judges. While speaking, be sure to point out any laboratory apparatus, charts, or photographs on display to reinforce your points.

Don't block the view of the judges. Let them see your exhibit by standing off to the side.

WHAT TO SAY

Begin by introducing yourself. Then give the title of your project, followed by an explanation of your purpose. Briefly summarize any background information and discuss how you developed an interest in the topic. Explain how you proceeded with your project, emphasizing any results or conclusions by pointing to graphs, charts, or tables in your exhibit. Be sure to mention any problems encountered in completing your project, and tell the judges how you overcame these obstacles.

If you did a laboratory investigation, go directly from your results to your conclusions. Again keep in mind that failure to support your hypothesis is perfectly acceptable. Tell the judges what applications your project has to other areas of science or its relevance to everyday situations. Comment on any ideas or suggestions for further research or ways to improve your project.

Finally, invite questions from the judges. Think before you answer. Speak slowly when talking to the judges. If you are asked a question you feel is not related to your project, tell them that you were not concerned with that particular area in your work. However, don't hesitate to say that you don't know the answer to a pertinent question. You can express your opinion or venture a guess, but admit to the judges that you are only giving your opinion or guessing. Any attempt to talk around a judge's question might be disastrous.

Be direct and honest in acknowledging any help and assistance you obtained in conducting your project. As professionals working in science and engineering, the judges are like detectives in their ability to determine how well you understand the nature and implications of your work. When you have finished your oral presentation, thank the judges for their time and interest.

WHAT JUDGES LOOK FOR

The judges are not looking to criticize your work. They realize you may have spent considerable time and effort to complete the project, so they are interested in what you have learned from it. They are especially looking for ways in which you have approached and conducted your project in a scientific manner.

Ideally, the judges should be more interested in promoting and fostering your interest in science than in evaluating your project for an award. As in all contests, however, the judges must choose winners and award prizes. Not everyone at the science fair may feel they received the recognition they deserved. You may be more understanding if you recognized some limitations imposed on judging at a science fair.

Consider the little time you have in which to impress the judges. You may have conducted your project over a period of several years, but you have no more than ten minutes to convey its importance to the judges. In addition, consider that only one person may judge your project at a local or regional fair. In larger competitions, a team of several judges may be used. These people are volunteers recruited from schools, universities, research centers, industries, hospitals, and government agencies.

When judging teams are organized, an attempt is made to match their background and expertise with the nature of the project. A doctor *should* judge a project investigating the effects of antibiotics on disease-causing organisms. An engineer *should* evaluate a project exploring new designs for airplane wings.

However, the selection of judging teams may be a matter of chance: the doctor may wind up judging the wing designs, while the engineer may question how the antibiotics were tested. As a result, an excellent project may not get recognized for its sophistication of design and quality of work. Keep in mind that judging is subjective, even though the judges have guidelines to follow. Judges may have personal preferences or preformed opinions. After all, judges are human. In any case, they may fail to give the proper recognition to a project. At the same time, most projects probably don't win prizes simply because "better" projects were around. The main thing, of course, is to do your best and not worry about trying to second-guess the judges.

JUDGING CRITERIA

Not all science fairs use a standardized scoring sheet for judging projects, nor do they adhere to the same point distribution for each category. Nonetheless, most judges evaluate the project in terms of five basic areas: (1) scientific content and application, (2) creativity and originality, (3) thoroughness, (4) skill, and (5) clarity. Within each area, a number of questions can be asked. The judges may rate each answer on a scale from 0 to 5, with 5 being the highest rating while a 0 indicates that the project failed completely to address the point.

Try to balance what the judges expect with what you can do within the limitations of your time, resources, and ability. In addition, you must not conduct the project solely to impress the judges. The project must reflect your interests and the need to please yourself. In that way, a natural enthusiasm for, and genuine pride in, your work will be evident.

SCIENTIFIC CONTENT AND APPLICATION

The judges will check to see if you approached your project scientifically. Did you state your hypothesis clearly? Was the question or problem sufficiently limited so that an answer or solution was possible? Hopefully, you narrowed the topic so that it could be investigated and explored in a reasonable time. Simply working on a difficult and complex problem without arriving at a solution is not impressive.

A good scientist can identify an intriguing problem capable of being solved within a reasonable time using the most technologically advanced equipment. In the case of a scientist, that time may require several years of concentrated work. In your case, the judges will realize your project must reflect your age, involvement in school and community activities, and available resources.

The judges will also question you on procedures and methods. Did you design and execute your plan so that you did not wander from your intended purpose? Did you clearly recognize and define all the variables? If controls were necessary, were they included and used correctly? Did you record sufficient data to support your conclusions? Were your data relevant to answering the question posed by the project?

Did you recognize the limitations of the data and see connections between the project and other areas? Did you include ideas or specific proposals for further research? Was your bibliography comprehensive, and did it cite scientific rather than consumer publications?

CREATIVITY AND ORIGINALITY

The judges may ask how the project originated—did you happen upon the idea from reading a textbook, talking to a scientist, or going through the literature? If the idea was the independent outcome of your work and effort, the judges will give appropriate credit for creativity. No penalty is imposed if you started your project by seeking the advice of a professional or reading the literature. On the other hand, no points for creativity are awarded for a rather impressive project copied from a textbook or developed entirely by someone else. A less sophisticated project that is genuinely your brainchild and work will get more credit for creativity.

Your project can receive credit for originality in several ways. Did you design your own procedures to perform some lab analysis? Perhaps you constructed a piece of equipment specifically for your project. Of course, you may need to construct a kit to carry out your project. You might purchase a kit to build a telescope to make observations on Halley's comet. In these circumstances, the judges would not penalize the project, since they recognize that the telescope is only a tool, and not the product of the project.

Any student can spend money to buy equipment, but creative students will devise their own. Such students are always coming up with new ways of answering old ideas. By the way, if your project involves some field of engineering, the judges may not give high marks for creativity to a device that is ingenious but inoperable. Although the design may reflect creativity and originality, the device should work.

Originality can also be displayed in your analysis of data. Was there another interpretation, other than the obvious one, of your data? Do conflicting results point to some new direction? Are additional experiments needed to answer problems raised by inconclusive data? Don't extend yourself too far, but use your imagination to suggest further experiments or discuss the application of your project to other areas.

THOROUGHNESS

The maximum points given for thoroughness are usually not as high as those awarded for the first two categories. The judges might ask whether you based your conclusions upon a single experiment or on enough repetitions to obtain sufficient data. They may examine your notebook to determine if you kept complete and accurate records for each experiment.

The judges may also question whether you used all possible approaches to test your hypothesis. You may be asked to comment on other theories concerning your project or additional ways of interpreting your data. They may look through your bibliography to see if you were thorough in your library research.

SKILL

Judges usually rate technical skill as important as thoroughness. They may ask questions to determine if you have all the design, laboratory, observational, analytical, and construction skills necessary to complete your project. Naturally, the judges will be interested in the amount of assistance provided by parents, teachers, scientists, and engineers. They may ask about the equipment used in your project: was it built independently, or was it part of a laboratory where you worked?

CLARITY

Finally, the judges will evaluate the clarity of your presentation and exhibit. How well did you explain and discuss your project? Obviously, this will reflect the extent to which you understand your investigation and its applications. Clearly explain your methods so that everyone can understand what you accomplished.

The judges will examine your exhibit. Were the important phases of the project presented logically and clearly, without resorting to flashy gimmicks or cute gadgets that detract more than they enhance?

Take the opportunity at the science fair to walk around and talk to other young scientists. See what they did, and you may get some ideas on how to improve your own project.

Remember, your project is not being judged for its special effects but rather for its scientific value.

MISSION ACCOMPLISHED

After making your presentation, the most anxious time has arrived—waiting for the announcement of winners. Winning is nice, but not everything. If you do not win any prizes at the fair, think what you have accomplished. You began with an idea, planned a project, explored the world of science, and built an exhibit to display your work.

If you don't receive an award, listen carefully to the judges' suggestions that might improve your project for the next science fair. More important, take the opportunity while you're at the fair to walk around and talk with other students. See what they did; you may get some good ideas for next year's project from this year's winners.

The experience of completing a project and exhibiting it for evaluation by professionals is worth your effort, no matter what the outcome. Approach your project as a learning experience, not as a way of winning a prize at a science fair. But we hope that if you have followed the suggestions offered in this book, the judges will make the same comment about your project as Holmes made about one of his investigations: "I think, Watson, that of all our cases we have had none more fantastic than this."

GLOSSARY

Abstract—a short detailed written description of a scientific research project.

Control—part of an experimental setup permitting only one independent variable to be present.

Control group—a test group used as the basis for comparison where no experimental factors are introduced.

Dependent variable—a factor in an experiment that is caused to change or is affected by a second factor under the experimenter's control.

Experimental group—a group subjected to the factor being tested in the investigation.

Hypothesis—a statement or idea to be proven or disproven by experimental testing.

Independent variable—the factor that the experimenter can change at will.

Invertebrates—animals without backbones, such as crabs, clams, caterpillars, and cockroaches.

Qualitative experiment—a procedure whereby observations, but not numerical results, are recorded.

Quantitative experiment—a procedure whereby measurements and numerical data are recorded.

Scientific method—a procedure often followed for carrying out an experiment that includes forming a hypothesis, designing the experimental steps, collecting data, and arriving at a conclusion.

Statistics—a branch of mathematics dealing with the analysis of numbers.

Vertebrates—animals with backbones, such as fish, frogs, finches, and humans.

BIBLIOGRAPHY

The following books have ideas for all types of projects, suggestions for carrying out your work, or tips on how to present your project.

Apfel, Necia, H. *Astronomy and Planetology: Projects for Young Scientists.* New York: Franklin Watts, 1983.

Beller, Joel. *Experimenting with Plants.* New York: Arco, 1985.

_____*So You Want to Do a Science Project!* New York: Arco, 1982.

Berman, William. *How to Dissect: Special Projects for Advanced Study.* New York: Arco, 1984.

Brown, Vinson. *Building Your Own Nature Museum for Study and Pleasure.* New York: Arco, 1985.

Byers, T.J. *20 Selected Solar Projects.* Englewood Cliffs, N.J.: Prentice-Hall, 1984.

Campbell, R. C. *Statistics for Biologists.* New York: Cambridge University Press, 1974.

Dunbar, Robert E. *The Heart and Circulatory System: Projects for Young Scientists.* New York: Franklin Watts, 1984.

Eakin, Richard M. *Great Scientists Speak Again.* Berkeley and Los Angeles: University of California Press, 1982.

Gardner, Martin. *Entertaining Science Experiments with Everyday Objects.* New York: Dover, 1981.

Gardner, Robert. *Ideas for Science Projects.* New York: Franklin Watts, 1986.

Gutnik, Martin A. *Ecology: Projects for Young Scientists.* New York: Franklin Watts, 1984.

_____*Genetics: Projects for Young Scientists.* New York: Franklin Watts, 1985.

MacFarlane, Ruth B. *Collecting and Preserving Plants for Science and Pleasure.* New York: Arco, 1985.

McKay, David A., and Bruce G. Smith. *Space Science Projects for Young Scientists.* New York: Franklin Watts, 1986.

Pawlicki, T.B., *How to Build a Flying Saucer and Other Proposals in Speculative Engineering.* Englewood Cliffs, N.J.: Prentice-Hall, 1981.

Peters, James A. *Classic Papers in Genetics.* Englewood Cliffs, N.J.: Prentice-Hall, 1959.

Photography in Your Science Fair Project. Rochester, N.Y.: Eastman Kodak Company, 1985.

Research Problems in Biology: Investigations for Students (3 volumes). Biological Sciences Curriculum Study. New York: Oxford University Press, 1976.

Rom, Harre. *Great Scientific Experiments: Twenty Experiments That Changed Our View of the World.* New York: Oxford University Press, 1983.

Schmidt, Victor E., and Verne N. Rockcastle. *Teaching Science with Every Day Things.* New York: McGraw-Hill, 1982.

Schulman, Elayne, Ken Craigo, William F. Griffiths, and Denise Megna. *Science Projects with Computers.* New York: Arco Publishing, 1985.

Science Fairs and Projects. National Science Teachers Association, 1985.

Smith, Norman. *How Fast Do Your Oysters Grow?* New York: Julian Messner, 1982.

Stong, C.L. *Scientific American Book of Projects for the Amateur Scientist.* New York: Simon and Schuster, 1960.

Stoodley, K.D. *Basic Statistical Techniques for Engineering & Science Students.* Woodstock, N.Y.: Beekman, 1974.

Tocci, Salvatore. *Chemistry Around You: Experiments and Projects with Everyday Products.* New York: Arco, 1985.

Trowbridge, Leslie W. *Experiments in Meteorology: A Book of Investigations for the Amateur Scientist.* New York: Doubleday, 1973.

University of Iowa General Chemistry Staff. *Experiments in Chemistry.* Champaign, Ill.: Stipes, 1981.

Van Deman, Barry A., and Ed McDonald. *Nuts and Bolts: A Matter of Fact Guide to Science Fair Projects.* Hammond Heights, Ill.: Science Man Press, 1980.

Vogt, Gregory. *The Space Shuttle: Projects for Young Scientists.* New York: Franklin Watts, 1983.

Wold, Allen L. *Computer Science: Projects for Young Scientists.* New York: Franklin Watts, 1984.

The following books provide a perspective on how people use both scientific and detective work in grappling with problems and arriving at solutions.

DeKruif, Paul. *Hunger Fighters.* New York: Harcourt Brace, 1967.

_____*Microbe Hunters.* New York: Harcourt Brace, 1966.

Doyle, Arthur Conan. *The Complete Sherlock Holmes.* New York: Doubleday, 1930. (Many other editions exist as well.)

Gregg, Charles T. *A Virus of Love and Other Tales of Medical Detection*. New York: Scribner, 1983.

Judson, Horace Freeland. *The Search for Solutions*. New York: Holt, Rinehart, 1980.

Roueché, Berton. *The Medical Detectives*. New York: Washington Square Press, 1982.

The following books provide information about Darwin's life and work.

Darwin, Charles. *The Voyage of The Beagle*. New York: Doubleday, 1962.

Miller, Jonathan, and Borin Van Loon. *Darwin for Beginners*. New York: Pantheon Books, 1982.

INDEX